D0093963

12 Faithful Women

PORTRAITS of STEADFAST ENDURANCE

EDITED by MELISSA KRUGER & KRISTEN WETHERELL

12 Faithful Women: Portraits of Steadfast Endurance
Copyright © 2020 by The Gospel Coalition

Published by The Gospel Coalition

The Gospel Coalition
P.O. Box 170346
Austin, Texas 78717

Cover design: Gabriel Reyes-Ordeix
Typesetting: Ryan Leichty

ISBN:
978-1-7334585-2-8 (paperback)
978-1-7334585-3-5 (ebook)
978-1-7334585-4-2 (kindle)

Printed in the United States of America

Ever since I was a little girl, my heart has been warmed and my faith fueled by biographies of faithful men and women of God. The portraits of godly women found in this collection will do the same for you. In each challenge and trial these women faced, Christ proved himself to be steadfast and sufficient. The courage and compassion they exhibited in their times are no less needed in ours. May their stories inspire us to reflect his majestic gospel and grace to our world.

NANCY DEMOSS WOLGEMUTH, founder and Bible teacher of *Revive Our Hearts* and author of *Adorned: Living Out the Beauty of the Gospel Together*

If you feel weary or worn, you don't need a change in circumstance; you need the testimony of God's faithfulness in the lives of believers who have persevered. *12 Faithful Women* points us to our faithful God, and in so doing, encourages our hearts to remain steadfast, right where we are.

RUTH CHOU SIMONS, founder of GraceLaced.com and best-selling author of *Beholding and Becoming* and *Foundations*

Those who profess faith in Jesus Christ are adopted into a family—a family that has spanned more than 2,000 years. It falls to each of us to get to know the members of our new family. Through this book, we can get to know and appreciate the unique contributions of 12 faithful women—12 faithful sisters in Christ.

TIM CHALLIES, blogger at challies.com and author of *Epic: An Around-the-World Journey through Christian History* and *Devoted: Great Men and Their Godly Moms*

Stories! Stories of women who have served Christ faithfully. Stories of saints who have suffered steadfastly. What a gift, these stories. This book helps light up the great and growing cloud of witnesses.

KATHLEEN NIELSON, speaker and author of *Women and God: Hard Questions, Beautiful Truth*

In *12 Faithful Women*, we're given glimpses of steadfastness in the midst of suffering. The various authors profile the lives of 12 women who show us, through their examples of endurance, how we too can be found faithful. If you want encouragement to walk fearlessly with God, pick up this book and let the lives of these godly women point the way.

COURTNEY DOCTOR, author of *From Garden to Glory: A Bible Study on the Bible's Story* and *Steadfast: A Devotional Bible Study on the Book of James*

Contents

Contributors

ABIGAIL DODDS (MA, Bethlehem College & Seminary) is a wife and mom of five children. She is a member at Bethlehem Baptist Church, where her husband, Tom, serves as an elder. Her favorite work includes excessive baking, gardening by hook or crook, and mediocre knitting. She is the author of *(A)Typical Woman* and a regular contributor at Desiring God.

K. A. ELLIS is passionate about theology, human rights, and global religious freedom. She is the director of the Edmiston Center for the Study of the Bible and Ethnicity at Reformed Theological Seminary in Atlanta, where she is also a Robert Cannada fellow for world Christianity. Since 2006, she has collaborated with the Swiss-based organization International Christian Response and travels internationally advocating for marginalized, overlooked, persevering Christians — both in history and also the contemporary world.

CHRISTINE HOOVER is a pastor's wife, mom of three boys, host of the By Faith podcast, and author of several books. Her latest offering is *With All Your Heart: Living Joyfully Through Allegiance to King Jesus*. Previous books include *Messy Beautiful Friendship*, *Searching for Spring*, and *From Good to Grace*. Originally from Texas, she and her family live in Charlottesville, Virginia, where they planted a church in 2008.

BETSY CHILDS HOWARD is an editor for The Gospel Coalition. She is the author of *Seasons of Waiting: Walking by Faith When Dreams Are Delayed* and the children's book *Arlo and the Great Big Cover-Up*. She and her husband, Bernard, live in Manhattan, where he is the pastor of Good Shepherd Anglican Church, which they planted in 2017.

JEN OSHMAN is a wife and mom to four daughters and has served as a missionary and pastor's wife for two decades on three continents. She currently resides in Colorado, where her family planted Redemption Parker. Her passion is leading women into a deeper faith and fostering a biblical worldview. Her first book is *Enough About Me: Find Lasting Joy in the Age of Self*.

CATHERINE PARKS lives in Nashville, Tennessee, with her husband, two children, and a cute dog named Ollivander. She's the author of four books, including *Real: The Surprising Secret to Deeper Relationships* and *Empowered* and *Strong*, collections of biographies for middle-grade readers.

KAREN SWALLOW PRIOR earned her PhD from the State University of New York at Buffalo. She is research professor of English and Christianity and culture at Southeastern Baptist Theological Seminary. She is the author of *Fierce Convictions — The Extraordinary Life of Hannah More: Poet, Reformer, Abolitionist*; *On Reading Well: Finding the Good Life through Great Books*; and *Booked: Literature in the Soul of Me*.

COURTNEY REISSIG is a writer and Bible teacher who has written for The Gospel Coalition, *The Washington Post*, and *Christianity Today*. She is author of three books: *Teach Me to Feel*, *Glory in the Ordinary*, and *The Accidental Feminist*. She is married to Daniel, and they are the proud parents of four sons. They make their home in Little Rock, Arkansas, where they serve at Immanuel Baptist Church.

VANEETHA RENDALL RISNER is a writer and speaker who is passionate about helping others find hope and joy in suffering. She is the author of the books *The Scars That Have Shaped Me: How God Meets Us in Suffering* and an upcoming memoir, *Walking Through Fire: A Memoir of Loss and Redemption*. Vaneetha is a regular contributor to Desiring God.

IRENE SUN was born in Malaysia. She is the author of the picture book *God Counts: Numbers in His Word and His World*. She studied liturgy and literature at Yale University (MAR) and the Old Testament at Trinity Evangelical Divinity School (ThM). She teaches her four boys at home with her preacher husband and through TGC's Women's Training Network.

REBECCA VANDOODEWAARD is a wife, mother, and author. Living south of her native Canada, she spends her time teaching, writing, and hosting along with her husband, a church history professor. Her books include *Reformation Women: Sixteenth-Century Figures Who Shaped Christianity's Rebirth* and the Banner of Truth board book series for children.

KRISTEN WETHERELL is a wife, mother, and writer. She is the author of *Fight Your Fears: Trusting God's Character and Promises When You Are Afraid* and the co-author of the award-winning book *Hope When It Hurts: Biblical Reflections to Help You Grasp God's Purpose in Your Suffering*. Kristen lives in Chicagoland with her husband, who is a pastor at The Orchard, and their daughter.

Introduction: Steadfast Under Trial

*Blessed is the man who remains steadfast under trial, for when
he has stood the test he will receive the crown of life, which
God has promised to those who love him.*

James 1:12

What is the hardest trial you have endured? Did you come out on
the other side the same as when you entered it? Probably not. Trials
have a way of changing us, for better or worse. They can humble us
or harden us. They can make us run to God or away from him. They
can cause us to ask profound and important questions about our
identity, purpose, and hope (or lack thereof), and about God — who
he is and what he might be doing.

A decade ago, I spent a year in New York City that changed
me. It brought one hard thing after another — loneliness, job loss,
heartbreak, financial stress, chronic pain. I remember thinking,
No more, Lord, please ... Yet, Jesus used those trials to exercise
and strengthen my faith — not in myself or my own understand-

1

ing, resolve, or strength, but in him, in his faithful character and steadfast purposes.

My circumstances in that season didn't immediately change for the better (in fact, they got worse in some ways). But my unchangeable God revealed himself to me within them. He awakened me to the reality of my dependence on him as Creator and Sustainer. He exposed my earthly hopes for the unreliable and unfulfilling idols they were and showed me that he is the only Savior worth worshiping. He convicted me that his Word of truth bolsters faith and battles fear. And he reminded me of his faithfulness displayed at the cross, where he proved his steadfast love and provided for my greatest eternal need.

Take a minute to think about your current situation. Maybe your life is smooth sailing, or perhaps the storms have been relentless. Maybe you trust in Jesus as your Savior, maybe you don't. Perhaps your trials have resulted in a closer walk with him, or maybe he seems far away. You might have questions about God's character, and your trials might have tempted you to doubt his goodness and purposes.

Whatever your situation, I hope you'll be both encouraged and also challenged by the stories within these pages. They are portraits of 12 faithful women who steadfastly endured many trials — including physical pain, persecution, infertility, loneliness, and oppression — and who, in their various sufferings, found Christ to be an all-sufficient Lord and Savior, steadfast, faithful, and true. Enter into the stories of Corrie ten Boom, Susannah Spurgeon, Esther Ahn Kim, Phillis Wheatley, Lilias Trotter, and others, and you'll see women who held fast to Jesus. They steadfastly endured not because of their own perfection or strength, but because Christ's strength was made perfect in their weakness (2 Cor. 12:9).

At the end of every chapter you'll find a section called "Lessons from the Faithful." There, we will summarize what we can learn from each woman's story. We will also offer some verses to read and provide several application questions to consider. Use these for personal reflection or to spur on discussion in a small-group setting.

Friend, whether you are walking closely with Christ or struggling to do so, he wants you to know an important truth, and it's what we hope you take away from this book:

Within your trials, knowing Jesus makes all the difference.

Romans 5 tells us why:

> We rejoice in our sufferings, knowing that suffering produces endurance, and endurance produces character, and character produces hope, and hope does not put us to shame, because God's love has been poured into our hearts through the Holy Spirit who has been given to us. For while we were still weak, at the right time Christ died for the ungodly. (Rom. 5:3–6)

The only way to steadfastly endure trials with hope is by keeping our eyes fixed upon the One who endured suffering and death for us so that we might live forever. We "[look] to Jesus, the founder and perfecter of our faith, who *for the joy that was set before him endured the cross*, despising the shame, and is seated at the right hand of the throne of God" (Heb. 12:2, italics added).

When we trust Christ by faith, receiving him as our Savior and our Lord, we have hope — hope within our trials and hope beyond our trials — because we have *him*. And this hope makes all the difference, as Jesus gives us both present courage and also eternal perspective to steadfastly endure until we "receive the crown of life, which God has promised to those who love him" (James 1:12).

Often, God fortifies our faith through the witness of steadfast Christians who've gone before us. The same God who walked with them, walks with us. Thankfully, "He does not faint or grow weary; his understanding is unsearchable. He gives power to the faint, and to him who has no might he increases strength" (Isa. 40:28–29).

May we learn from these 12 faithful women what it looks like to trust and follow Jesus so we might do the same.

Kristen Wetherell
Editor

Helen Roseveare: Steadfast in Sacrifice

BETSY CHILDS HOWARD

The mother died in childbirth, leaving behind a premature newborn and a 2-year-old daughter. Keeping the baby warm was essential for its survival. With no incubator or electricity, the hospital relied on hot water bottles to warm newborns, but their last bottle had burst. Helen and her staff managed to keep the baby alive through the night by having one of the midwives sleep with it next to the fire.

The next day, Helen gathered the orphans who lived at the mission for a time of prayer. She told them about the baby and the big sister, and the need for the baby to stay warm in order to survive. She asked them to pray, but was thrown by the prayer of 10-year-old Ruth: "Please God, send us a hot water bottle. It'll be no good tomorrow, God, as the baby'll be dead; so please send it this after-noon. And while you are at it, would you please send a dolly for the little girl, so she'll know you really love her?"

While this prayer may not sound audacious to us, Helen knew that it was a near-impossible request. There were no pharmacies selling hot water bottles anywhere close to Nebobongo. Helen wrote, "The only way God *could* answer this particular prayer would be by sending me a parcel from the homeland. I had been in Africa almost four years at that time, and I had never, never received a parcel from home; anyway, if anyone *did* send me a parcel, who would put in a hot water bottle? I lived on the equator."

Much to Helen's surprise, a large box from England — the first she had ever received — arrived on her doorstep that very afternoon. She called to her the orphans who had prayed that morning, and they opened the package together. Carefully, she untied the string and removed the paper while the children's anticipation grew.

The box contained colorful knitted jerseys and bandages for hospital patients. There was soap and a box of raisins. Then Helen reached in and pulled out a hot water bottle. She couldn't help crying as she realized how small her faith had been. Little Ruth immediately announced, "If God has sent the bottle, He must have sent the dolly too!" Sure enough, the last thing in the box was a beautiful baby doll. The package had been on its way for five months before Ruth prayed her prayer.[1]

. . .

Helen Roseveare was born in 1925 to a well-educated, but not especially well-off, English family. The Roseveare family was moderately religious. Helen attended Sunday school and was confirmed in the Church of England. Yet her inherited faith didn't answer her questions about the meaning of life or absolve her guilt over her sins.

Helen chose to study medicine at Cambridge University, and the need for war-time doctors put her on an accelerated track. From the first day she was there, evangelical Christian students reached out to her as a friend. She began studying the Bible with them — once staying up all night reading the book of Romans — and finally trusted Christ as her Savior.

1   Helen Roseveare, *Living Faith* (Fearn, Ross-shire: Christian Focus, 2016), 56–58.

The next few years were joyful ones as Helen grew in her faith and saw others come to Christ through her witness (including the leader of the Cambridge University Women's Communist Party!). After Cambridge, she completed her medical training at West London Hospital.

Helen felt called to practice medicine on the mission field, and so in 1953, she sailed to the Congo,[2] where she would work as a missionary doctor for the next 20 years.

AFRICAN MISSION

Helen began her career in the Congo at the Ibambi mission station. Since there was no other doctor, she immediately started seeing patients, in spite of many language barriers. Her day would begin with tea at 5 a.m. followed by communal morning prayer and Bible study. She began seeing patients at 9 a.m., and described her days this way:

> Noise, heat, smells, waves of nausea, everyone talking at once, crying babies, running sores ... it was dusk before all had drifted away and I was left cleaning the room, sorting out what there was of drugs, frantically making lists of what we urgently needed, almost overcome by waves of weariness and in the background a slight dread of inability to cope.[3]

2   From 1876 to the present, the country in which Helen Roseveare ministered has been known by five different names: the Congo Free State, the Belgian Congo, Republic of Congo-Léopoldville, the Republic of Zaire, and the Democratic Republic of Congo (its current name). For simplicity's sake, I refer to the region simply as "the Congo."

3   Helen Roseveare, *Give Me This Mountain* (Fearn, Ross-shire: Christian Focus, 2006), 75.

In the beginning, Helen had no helper, and she quickly realized she needed to train nurses. Helen thrived as a teacher. She would later say that teaching was a much more natural calling for her than medicine. Medicine left her depleted; teaching energized her.

Life in the Congo was hard. Helen often had to drive many miles to villages, and more often than not her vehicle would break down or get stuck in the mud, sometimes in the middle of the night. There were all kinds of bugs, including a stinging red fly that infected Helen with painful parasites. No treatment was ever successful at curing them, so she lived with them for the rest of her life.

Toward the end of her first year in Africa, a man showed up at Helen's door and told her that he had come to be her cook. He had had to leave his previous employment because he was infected with leprosy.

Although Helen was not afraid of leprosy, her heart sank at the thought of all it would entail to treat a leper. There was still a huge stigma against leprosy, to the point that lepers would have to be treated in a separate building with separate equipment. She was already working 18 hours a day! However, God wouldn't let her refuse. They built a small mud-and-thatch building to be the leprosy clinic and ordered supplies of leprosy drugs.

The bill for the medicine came to 4,320 Belgian francs. Helen didn't have the money to pay the bill, but she figured since God was the one who had moved her to treat leprosy patients, he would supply the money. She put the bill in her Bible and waited, but no money came. It was mission policy that all bills must be paid by the end of the month. That day came, but still no money. Helen didn't even have a reserve to draw from. She felt aggrieved that God had not provided the funds for this work that he had thrust upon her.

Then, mid-day, someone brought Helen an envelope addressed to her. It was three different donations. The total amount was 4,800 Belgian francs. Helen calculated that, minus a tithe of 480 francs, she would have the exact amount to pay the bill for the medicine — 4,320 francs. The gift had been en route from North America for four months. Two of the donations had been marked "for your leprosy work." At the time they were sent, Helen had no plans to work with lepers! [4]

In 1955, when Helen had been in the Congo for a couple of years, she met another doctor who had a vision for creating a specialized hospital for leprosy. They decided that it would be ideal to combine the nurse training program (overseen by her) with a leprosy hospital. Helen assumed this would all be built at her beloved Ibambi mission center where she had invested two years creating a functioning clinic, a 32-bed hospital, and a medical dispensary. She was dismayed and incensed when the mission leaders told her they wanted her to move her nurse's training school seven miles away to Nebobongo where they had a small mission orphanage. It would mean starting over. Helen fumed and argued with the committee, but eventually she prayed and submitted to the decision to build a new hospital and nurses training school at Nebobongo.

This move required hard, physical labor. The buildings they occupied had lain vacant for two years, and the jungle had taken over. Helen hauled bricks from the kiln and negotiated with local suppliers for building materials. The manual labor made it difficult for her to start training nurses or seeing patients. She felt resentful and asked some of the African Christians to pray for her. After praying, one of the men spoke up:

> "Doctor," he said, "when you are being a doctor, in your white coat, stethoscope round your neck, speaking French, you are miles from us. We fear you and all say: 'Yes, yes,' hardly even hearing what you said. But when you are down at the kiln with us, and your hands are rough as ours are, when you are out at the markets using our language and making howlers and we all laugh at you; that's when we love you, and how we have

4   Helen Roseveare, *Living Fellowship* (Fearn, Ross-shire: Christian Focus, 2016), 55–56.

9

come to trust you and can listen to what you tell us of God and His ways."[5]

This response humbled Helen and opened her eyes to the ways God could use what she considered a distraction to make her a more effective missionary. Eventually, Helen was able to concentrate on medicine again, and the hospital at Nebobongo flourished.

In addition to doing surgery and training nurses, once a week Helen would drive 60 miles to Wamba to get supplies. One week, Helen arrived home from her supply trip exhausted. It was after 10 p.m., but someone had left a plate of dinner for her. She consumed one mouthful and decided she was too tired to eat, so she gave the rest to the dog that was at her feet begging for food. Later that night she became violently ill. The next morning, one of her helpers found the dog dead on the floor and Helen delirious. She had been poisoned, and then while she suffered, her poisoners stole everything they could from her house.[6]

This kind of thing happened a lot to Helen and can evoke two different responses. The first is amazement at God's protection. If Helen had eaten the whole meal, it would have been her rather than the dog who had died. On the other hand, why did God let Helen get robbed? She had worked so hard and sacrificed so much. Surely God could have spared her this trial!

Helen believed that God allowed these hugely inconvenient trials to give her opportunities to "count it all joy" no matter what her circumstances. She knew that someday she might, in hindsight, see God's purpose, but she needed to give thanks in the present. This was not easy for her, but she did it. Her thanksgiving was interspersed with tears, but she chose to rejoice in the Lord by faith.

---

5   Helen Roseveare, *Living Sacrifice* (Fearn, Ross-shire: Christian Focus, 2013), 80.

6   Alan Burgess, *Daylight Must Come: The Story of Dr. Helen Roseveare* (London: Michael Joseph, 1975), 155.

FAITHFULLY SINGLE

When Helen left for the mission field, she knew that she might never marry. During most days in the Congo, she was too busy to be lonely. But by the time she went on her first furlough in 1958, Helen was tired of being single on the mission field. She told God that she wanted to return to the Congo with a nice surgeon for a husband. She wanted someone to help shoulder the responsibility and undertake the physical labor usually reserved for men that so often fell to Helen.

While doing some additional medical training in England, she met a devoted Christian doctor. He seemed to be an ideal fit for her plans, except that he didn't have a call to the mission field. Gradually, Helen's desire shifted from wanting to return to the Congo with a husband to simply wanting this man to be her husband. She asked God to release her from her missionary call.

During this time, Helen's spiritual life dried up. She knew she was following her own desires at the expense of the calling from which God had not yet released her. Finally, she surrendered to God's leading. She and her suitor agreed not to see each other again.[7]

Helen went back to Africa at peace. Although she may have had a right to marry, she had laid that right down. She had wanted a husband so that she could "pass the buck" to someone, but she sensed that God was saying, "Pass the buck to me."[8] In later years, when asked how she handled her singleness, she would respond that she was in love with Jesus. He was her protector and keeper. She didn't *always* feel resigned to singleness — there were times when she very much wanted physical arms around her — but she always found God faithful.

7 Roseveare, *Give Me This Mountain*, 116.
8 Helen Roseveare, "The Cost of Declaring His Glory." *Urbana 76*. Accessed November 2019.

WAR IN THE CONGO

When Helen became a Christian, a Bible teacher had written Philippians 3:10 in her Bible: "That I may know him, and the power of his resurrection, and the fellowship of his sufferings, being made conformable unto his death." On that winter day in 1945, neither he nor Helen realized just how deeply she would know the fellowship of Christ's suffering.

The Congo had been a Belgian colony since 1908, but in 1960, it was declared independent. The leadership vacuum left various people and parties vying for power. Independence brought on a series of crises, assassinations, and regime changes that lasted for five years. In 1964, the conflict known as the Simba rebellion broke out in Helen's region. Fighting raged between two groups of Africans, the Congolese National Army and the Simba guerillas.

The missionaries at Ibambi and Nebobongo were caught by surprise. They had grown used to unrest in the country since independence, but it hadn't hindered their work. They realized this time it was different when Simba rebels arrived at their hospital as an occupying army.

Helen and the other hospital workers were at the mercy of the guerillas. Many of these were adolescent boys who had been conscripted into the army. Helen described their captors as "brutal and drunken. They cursed and swore, they struck and kicked, they used the butt-end of rifles and rubber truncheons."[9]

Helen's most severe ordeal of her captivity happened on the night of October 29, 1964. Around 2:30 a.m., a group of soldiers forced their way into her cottage. Two male nurses had been sleeping in her front room as bodyguards, but there was nothing they could do to keep the soldiers out. Simba rebels ransacked the house, smashing whatever they didn't steal. Finally, when she thought they were leaving, the lieutenant, the leader of the pack, commanded her

9   Roseveare, *Give Me This Mountain*, 145.

to go into the bedroom and get undressed. Instead, she ran outside and tried to hide in the bush. They found her and dragged her back in. One of the male nurses fought to protect her and was beaten unconscious. Then the lieutenant raped her.

In that moment, Helen felt completely deserted by God, lifting up her own cry of "My God, my God, why have you forsaken me?" And God answered her. These are her words from her book *Living Sacrifice*:

> In the darkness and loneliness, He met with me. He was right there, a great, wonderful, almighty God. His love enveloped me. Suddenly the "Why?" dropped away from me, and an unbelievable peace flowed in, even in the midst of the wickedness. And He breathed a word into my troubled mind: the word *privilege*.
>
> "These are not your sufferings: they are not beating you. These are My sufferings: all I ask of you is the loan of your body."[10]

Helen experienced a peace that passes understanding. She didn't attribute her suffering to a God who was two-faced and angry, or one who was unable to protect her. Instead, she saw that the same loving Savior who had meticulously provided a hot water bottle and doll to two baby orphans had allowed her to suffer for him, and she considered that suffering a privilege.

In the miserable months that followed, Helen didn't always *feel* peace. She felt frightened and hopeless many times. But each time she kept walking by faith, returning to her hope that the man of sorrows, well-acquainted with grief, was her companion and would not let her suffer in vain.

Eventually, the missionaries were removed from Nebobongo and imprisoned, along with a group of nuns, at a Roman Catholic convent. Helen was held captive for a total of five months. Finally, it

10   Roseveare, *Living Sacrifice*, 22.

became apparent that the Simbas in charge of Helen's group were on the run. They moved their prisoners with them as front-line hostages. While they were on the move, Helen was raped a second time.[11] But a few days later, on New Year's Eve 1964, they were rescued by international mercenary troops.

Helen flew home to England, where she spent the next 14 months traveling, speaking, and writing her first memoir, *Give Me This Mountain*. She devoted only seven pages to talking about the Simba rebellion, and does not mention the rapes. She was still too traumatized at that point and not ready to relive it.

RETURN TO THE MISSION

The decision over whether to return to the Congo was a hard one for Helen. In addition to the trauma of her last five months in Africa, there had previously been some racial tensions among hospital staff. *Would they even want her to come back?* Helen wondered.

Then letters started arriving that convinced her she was not only needed but earnestly desired. One student wrote, "Don't blame us, Doctor, for all that has happened, but pity us for all we suffer. Come back, please! We are waiting for you expectantly. As God enables us, we will see it never happens again."[12]

And so, in March 1966, Helen Roseveare returned to the Congo. What she found was devastating. Although the people enthusiastically welcomed her back, 90 percent of all that had been built at Nebobongo had been destroyed by the Simba army.[13] The people living there lacked food, medicine, and even clothes. Helen took on

---

11 Helen Roseveare, *He Gave Us a Valley* (Fearn, Ross-shire: Christian Focus, 2006), 39; Burgess, *Daylight Must Come*, 195–196.

12 Ibid., 47.

13 Helen Roseveare, *Digging Ditches* (Fearn, Ross-shire: Christian Focus, 2012), 15.

the work of relief and rebuilding, finding agencies to donate food, clothing, medicine, and building supplies by the truck load.

Even as work to restore Nebobongo was underway, Helen was thinking about the future. She had an offer from another doctor at Nyankunde, an area 450 miles away, to build a 250-bed training hospital as a cooperative effort of five mission organizations. Helen had always said, "No white man is justified in working in Black Africa unless he/she is teaching."[14] The hospital at Nyankunde would multiply the numbers of Africans she would be able to train. So she started over again.

Although they had been given land for the hospital, they did not have housing for students or money to build it. Helen, impatient to get started, was unwilling to waste a year in fundraising and then building. Instead, she spread the word that qualified students desiring to be trained should arrive the first week of August.

Twenty-two students showed up expecting to start classes. To their great surprise, they found no buildings. Helen informed them that they must first build the training school. "You build, I teach," she said. The new students were understandably aggrieved. They had come for an education, not to do manual labor. The students grumbled, but they worked hard. They felled trees and dug toilets. Whatever work the students did, Helen did along with them. Three months later, Helen held her first class in her new training college.

Helen faced many interpersonal difficulties at Nyankunde. In her writing, Helen is honest about her own sin. Time after time in her books, she admits her own struggles with pride. Her honesty challenges her readers by suggesting that what we often label "hurt" may be pride in disguise. She writes:

When you feel hurt, stop and pray ... '[H]urt' means that the self is very much alive, and striving to get back on the throne of my life. If Jesus really indwells me, I ought not to be hurt. I may

14 Roseveare, *He Gave Us a Valley*, 93.

well be grieved at the behavior of others, or by certain events, but not hurt. Hurt is a symptom of self. If I let the Lord have His rightful place on the throne of my life, He will handle that which causes the hurt.[15]

After seven years at Nyankunde, Helen discerned that God was calling her back to England. Her mother's health was not good, and she felt she owed it to her siblings to share the burden of her mother's care.[16] Multiple bouts of tropical fever had worn down Helen's own health, and, in her words, "[M]y own nervous energy was running low, so often tested as it was by mindless bureaucracy or sometimes brutal harassment."[17]

Helen's honesty and self-disclosure is one of the things that made her a popular speaker in later life. She wasn't the kind of missionary who seemed naturally holier than everyone around her. Dying to herself didn't come any easier to her than it does to any of us. Helen leaned into sanctification, allowing God to whittle her into his arrow.

Helen Roseveare left a rich legacy through her books, through missionaries sent out after hearing her speak, and through the medical training centers she founded in the Congo that are still functioning today. Over and over again, in her books and talks, Helen would use the word "privilege." It was a privilege to minister in the name of Christ and to suffer for him. She fought the good fight, kept the faith, and passed into eternity on December 7, 2016, at the age of 91.

15   Roseveare, *Digging Ditches*, 134.
16   Ibid., 17.
17   Ibid.

LESSONS FROM THE FAITHFUL

What we can learn about steadfast endurance from Helen Roseveare

CONSIDER HOW DISTRACTIONS MAY BE GIFTS FROM GOD.
Helen Roseveare felt frustrated whenever her plans were interrupted. Yet, time and again, she saw God work good purposes through something that felt like a waste of her time.

The next time you're sidelined from what you consider your calling, believe that God has a purpose for what you view as a distraction. Just as all of the manual building labor Helen did over the years opened the hearts of her African colleagues to love her, God can use detours from our own plans to accomplish things we don't expect.

Read Romans 8:28–29. What is the "good" God works in "those who love him"? This verse is likely familiar, and you may have applied it to your biggest struggles. In what ways can you also apply it to small, daily frustrations? How should you respond the next time your plans get interrupted by what seems like a distraction?

TRUST GOD WITH YOUR REPUTATION AND RELATIONSHIPS.
Helen was often hurt by her co-laborers in ministry. Yet, instead of nursing her wounds, she tried to see occasions where she felt hurt as opportunities for God to reveal her pride to her.

When you feel hurt, ask God to reveal your pride to you. Grieve, but entrust your reputation and relationships to him.

Read Philippians 2:5–8. Describe Jesus's example of humility. How should his example inform your response the next time you feel hurt by a Christian brother or sister?

CLING TO GOD WHEN HE LEADS YOU DOWN A PATH OF SUF-FERING. Many people wonder whether their faith will survive great suffering. Yet it is often in our darkest moments when we most know our need for God. Helen's immense suffering drove her into her Father's arms because she knew him to be the Healer. She knew there was nowhere else she could go.

Read John 6:66–69. What is Peter's reasoning behind cling-ing to Jesus? No matter what circumstances might befall us, if we are looking for "the words of eternal life," there is nowhere else for us to go but to Jesus. Write out a prayer that God will hold you fast in the day of suffering.

Esther Ahn Kim: Steadfast in Persecution

CATHERINE PARKS

Shivering in her jail cell and huddled together with fellow prisoners for warmth, Ahn Ei Sook (later known by her married name, Esther Ahn Kim) heard a moaning sound coming from a nearby cell. She inquired of a guard and was told it was coming from a 20-year-old Chinese woman who had brutally murdered her husband. The woman was said to be insane; she wore clothes that were always soiled, and her hands were tied behind her back since she refused to stop pounding on the door. The jailer said, "She is a real devil; she isn't even human."[1]

Ei Sook thought how cold this young woman must be, sitting alone with her hands tied. She thought of Jesus: "He healed and saved the sinners and the sick. If He were here, whom would He have

---

1   Esther Ahn Kim, *If I Perish* (Chicago: Moody Publishers, 1997), 172.

visited first? Me? He would have passed by my cell to visit and help the insane woman. She was the one who needed Him the most."[2]

Unable to stop thinking of the woman, Ei Sook prayed that she would be brought to her cell. Eventually the jailer agreed, and the prisoner was brought to Ei Sook's cell, where she instantly tried to bite her cellmates. She and Ei Sook fell into a wrestling match, with the Chinese woman violently trying to get free from Ei Sook's grasp. Finally, she collapsed onto the floor from exhaustion and fell asleep with her cold feet against Ei Sook's chest for warmth.

For three days, the young woman slept. Her stench filled the cell, and her snoring kept the other prisoners awake. Ei Sook prayed for guidance, later writing,

> Jesus Himself was participating in this battle, I realized. Surely my gratitude was beyond words. By nature, I would have tried to ignore the girl with all my might, but in reality exactly the opposite was happening. Here I was, holding a woman who was unspeakably dirty. Only Jesus' mercy could cause me to do it.
>
> Jesus knew I was selfish, weak, deceitful, and sinful. But He treated me as valuable and important. How could I avoid her simply because she was so dirty in my eyes? To Him, we were the same.[3]

Once a Christian school teacher, Ei Sook could never have foreseen her imprisonment in a Japanese cell. But the same powerful God who had carried her thus far would continue to work in the trying days ahead.

. . .

2   Ibid.
3   Ibid., 174.

Ahn Ei Sook was born in Korea on June 24, 1908. Two years later, after years of war, the Empire of Japan annexed Korea, making it part of Japan for the next 35 years. To force Koreans to assimilate to Japanese rule, Imperial Japan radically changed the Korean way of life. Speaking Korean in school was forbidden — art, film, and public life were also to be conducted in Japanese. In an attempt to erase the history of Korea, more than 200,000 Korean historical documents were destroyed. Even Korean names were eventually outlawed, and Koreans were assigned Japanese names instead.[4]

Japanese families moved to Korea, living on land taken from Koreans. In exchange, Koreans were forced to work in Japan by the hundreds of thousands, and during World War II, Korean women were forced into sexual slavery as "comfort women," existing only to satisfy the lust of military men.[5]

Assimilation reached into religion as well. Christianity was a growing movement in early 20th century Korea, and while it composed only 2 percent of the population in 1945, Korean Christians brought about advancements in medical care and education, opening hundreds of schools around the country.[6] Under Japanese rule, Koreans were forced to worship at Shinto shrines and pray to Japanese gods, dead emperors, and former war heroes. Those who refused, citing the commandment to have no gods other than Yahweh, were sent to prison for their disloyalty to the Empire.[7]

Ei Sook's family was divided. Her mother followed Christ, and her father's family practiced idol worship. As a child, Ei Sook hated seeing her grandmother worship idols and wondered how someone so religious could still be miserable. On one religious festival day,

4   Erin Blakemore, "How Japan Took Control of Korea," History.com, February 27, 2018, http://history.com/news/japan-colonization-korea/.

5   Blakemore, "How Japan Took Control of Korea."

6   James H. Grayson, *Korea: A Religious History* (London: RoutledgeCurzon, 2002), 169.

7   Donald N. Clark, *Culture and Customs of Korea* (Westport: Greenwood Press, 2000), 49.

Ei Sook sneaked into the room where they kept the food that was to be sacrificed to the idols, yelling at the false gods, "Why do you eat the best foods and then make my grandmother unhappy? Die eating the food mixed with my spittle!" She spat on her finger and rubbed her saliva all over the food. But this wasn't enough; she then put horse dung on the end of a walking stick and touched it to each idol basket, saying, "You demons! Why can't you make happiness and peace? Why do you make Grandmother unpleasant and upset while she worships you? Eat horse droppings and die!"[8]

One night before young Ei Sook fell asleep, her mother spoke to her about the difference between the God of the Bible and the idols her husband's family worshiped. Ei Sook had noticed the misery of idol worshipers compared to the quiet peace and happiness of her mother. Her mother said, "As you can see, idols have no power at all. The Lord Jesus is the only One who can give us true power and happiness and peace."[9] Ei Sook's mother, the daughter of a high government official in Seoul, had trusted Christ at 8 years old through the work of a missionary. Seeing her mother's faith in Christ, Ei Sook also trusted him and followed Jesus.

NO OTHER GOD

Ei Sook's mother wanted her daughter to attend a mission school. But her father insisted she receive a Japanese education, first at a public school in Korea, and then at a college in Japan. She studied in the Japanese language, becoming fluent and growing to love the Japanese people — but she couldn't have imagined how God would use this knowledge and love in later years.

After finishing her education in Japan, she came home to Korea and taught music at a Christian school. At that time, shrines had

8   Esther Ahn Kim, *If I Perish*, 95.
9   Ibid., 96.

been placed in every school, government office, home, and Christian church. The police had begun appearing at church services to make sure that every person bowed to the Shinto god before the service began. One day, the Japanese leaders took everyone from Ei Sook's school and the surrounding community to the local shrine, where they were forced to bow to a Japanese god. If they refused, the school would be closed, and they would be tortured.

As she walked to the shrine with her students, Ei Sook remembered how Shadrach, Meshach, and Abednego had refused to bow to the statue of the Babylonian king, Nebuchadnezzar. They knew God had the power to deliver them — but they also knew that even if he didn't, they would still not bow. They would honor God unto death, and Ei Sook decided she would do the same. "Today on the mountain, before the large crowd," she silently prayed, "I will proclaim that there is no other God beside You. This is what I will do for Your holy name."[10]

When the order came for everyone to bow to the sun goddess, the massive crowd obeyed — except for Ei Sook. As she thought about the torture to come as punishment for her disobedience, she remembered the words of a hymn:

Did we in our own strength confide,
        Our striving would be losing;
Were not the right Man on our side,
        The Man of God's own choosing:
Dost ask who that may be?
        Christ Jesus, it is He; Lord Sabaoth His Name,
From age to age the same,
        And He must win the battle.[11]

10   Ibid., 14.
11   Martin Luther, "A Mighty Fortress Is Our God."

When she returned to the school, four detectives were waiting for her. God gave her peace as they arrested her and took her to the district chief. But in the middle of his angry speech, the phone rang, and he rushed from the office. Ei Sook quickly got up, ran out of the building, and returned to her home. She had been given the gift of time to prepare for the trials to come. She packed a bag and left, going into hiding.

As she rode on a train through the night, she gazed at the stars shining brightly against the black sky. "True faith should be like those stars," she thought, "shining even brighter as the world becomes darker." She prayed that she would be able "to shine in the black night sky of my beloved country like a changeless star."[12]

MINISTRY TO JAPAN

While in hiding, Ei Sook was not idle. She spent her days preparing for her arrest and imprisonment. Knowing she would have no access to a Bible in prison, she committed more than 100 Bible chapters and many hymns to memory. She also fasted from food and water for days at a time and slept in the cold, preparing her body and mind for the harsh conditions of prison.

After a time of hiding in the country, the Lord led her to the city of Pyongyang. When she arrived, she saw a train loaded with young Japanese soldiers headed for the battlefields in China. Gazing into their empty eyes, Ei Sook had a strong sense that someone must go to the Japanese leaders and tell them how they were sending these young men to death and hell.

While in Pyongyang, Ei Sook met with many other Christians. They came and went in secret, some having been recently released from prison — but all of them knew prison might be in their futures. As they heard about the torture and persecution fellow believers had

12   Esther Ahn Kim, *If I Perish*, 22, 25.

faced, Ei Sook and others cried over what they might be forced to endure. She, like many others, had believed a miracle might occur to spare them either imprisonment or the pains of torture. But as she listened to accounts of brutal persecution, she realized she must be prepared to suffer and even die in obedience to God.

One day, a stranger named Elder Park came to her house and told her how God had commanded him to go to Pyongyang to see her. He said:

> "Everyone is so afraid that no one warns Japan. I have already been chosen by His holy voice. You have been chosen, too, haven't you?"
>
> Ei Sook was startled and afraid to speak.
>
> "You speak Japanese, don't you?" Elder Park asked.
>
> "Yes," she responded.
>
> "That is what we need: your good Japanese. But I have come to understand that you are a beautiful believer. What good can your excellent language do without faith? God has led me here so that He can use you."[13]

Despite this God-ordained encounter, Ei Sook looked for excuses to avoid Japan. She knew that going could mean torture or even death. She wanted God to give her a clear sign that she should go, so she came up with a test to determine his plan. Seeing the unbiblical way she was testing God, Ei Sook's mother told her it was wrong and dangerous to ask God for what the Bible doesn't say. "The Bible is our guide," she said.[14]

So Ei Sook fasted, prayed, and read her Bible for three days. She knew God was calling her to Japan, and she knew that to be beaten, starved, or killed would be better than to disobey him. She would go with Elder Park, come what may.

13   Ibid., 58.
14   Ibid., 61.

As the pieces fell into place, Ei Sook considered the sovereign plan of God who had controlled even her unbelieving father's plans, which included a Japanese education and instilled in her a God-given love for Japan. She was able to communicate with the Japanese leaders, she was familiar with Tokyo, and she had a deep love for the Japanese people.

Yet the path would be dangerous. Elder Park couldn't get a passport to travel to Japan because he had previously been a prisoner. While this worried Ei Sook, Elder Park had no fear. He knew God would make a way for them to do what he had called them to do. As God miraculously caused police to pass right over Elder Park on the train, Ei Sook's faith grew. The same thing happened when they boarded a ship. God was making their path straight. This did not mean it would be easy or smooth, but he would enable them to accomplish his purposes.

Ei Sook came to understand that the Japanese people, and even many of the country's leaders, didn't know how new Japanese military leaders were treating Koreans and Christians, in particular. Ei Sook and Elder Park were given unprecedented opportunities to meet with some of the leaders and warn them about God's judgment. They told these leaders they had a message from God: Japan would suffer his judgment by fire falling from the sky if they did not turn from their sin against him and his people.

While these meetings were encouraging, none had achieved the goal of bringing the situation in Korea to light before the leaders of Imperial Japan. However, Elder Park and Ei Sook saw an opportunity in the convening of the Imperial Diet, where all the highest officials in Japan would gather for legislative meetings. The two were, amazingly, granted admittance to the Diet, where the rules for attending were strict in order to avoid disturbances. But in the middle of the assembly, Elder Park dropped a sign from the balcony. On it, he had written a message calling the Japanese government to repent and withdraw from Korea and to examine which was the true religion — Shintoism or Christianity. Immediately, Elder Park and Ei Sook were arrested.

GRACE IN PRISON

From 1939 to 1945, Ei Sook lived in a Japanese prison in Pyongyang. The number "57" replaced her name. Ei Sook prayed, "The rest of the world has completely disappeared from me. I am a weakling. Unless I live each day holding Your hand, I'll become too frightened. Lord, hold my hand firmly so I won't part from You. Jesus, I love You."[15]

Over the next six years, Ei Sook encountered joy and sorrow in abundance. She and her fellow prisoners were constantly hungry, faced extreme cold, and were frequently yelled at by harsh and hateful female jailers. But the Lord also brought jailers who loved Ei Sook and became Christians. One such woman, Jue, approached her because she was curious about Christianity. She wanted to learn from pastors and knew that most of them were in jail, so she got a job at the prison to learn more about the Christian faith.

Repeatedly, Ei Sook cried out to God for strength, knowing how weak and incapable she was apart from his help. Many of Ei Sook's fellow prisoners trusted Christ because of her love for them and the witness of her faith. She loved the unlovable — the angry, dirty, proud, and insane. One such prisoner was the young Chinese woman facing execution for murdering her husband.

As she continued to care for her, Ei Sook told this woman that she loved her, and as she did, a miracle happened within her heart — she realized she loved, and even *liked*, this woman! She shared her food, combed the woman's tangled hair, and massaged her body. She told her of the love of Jesus and his offer of forgiveness.

15   Ibid., 141.

Over time, the jailers noticed a change in the young prisoner. When the executioners came for her, they did not have to use handcuffs. Having received the peace of Christ, she walked forward in faith. Ei Sook wrote,

> Without wiping the tears which were streaming down my cheeks, I watched her depart. Without fear, she put death aside and walked. It was exactly as when Jesus conquered death.
> "Death is swallowed up in victory. O death, where is thy victory? O grave, where is thy sting? The sting of death is sin; and the power of sin is the law: but thanks be to God, who giveth us the victory through our Lord Jesus Christ" (1 Corinthians 15:54–57).[16]

Through her six years in prison, God worked many miracles of salvation through Ei Sook's quiet, humble faith. In her suffering, the incarnation of Christ became sweeter to her; she knew that he had shared in her humanity and knew what it was to be cold, hungry, tortured, and despised. As she made hard sacrifices, like giving her meager meals to fellow prisoners, she rejoiced at the role she had been given:

> I wondered if I had ever experienced the worth of being a human being so much as now. It was an unbelievable privilege for a person like me, sinful, selfish, conceited, and with many faults, to receive an order from God, who was the Lord of the heavens and earth. I was overwhelmed. In spite of my weakness and sinfulness, the Lord had given me the grace to walk and work with Him.[17]

16   Ibid., 180.
17   Ibid., 213–214.

On August 15, 1945, Japan surrendered, and the prisoners were soon released. Upon her release, Ei Sook learned that fire had indeed rained down upon Japan from atomic bombs and that entire cities were aflame. She grieved for the many Japanese who had died without hearing the gospel and wondered what had become of the leaders who had ignored and laughed at her warnings.

SUPERNATURAL POWER

After her release from prison, Ei Sook moved to the United States to attend seminary, where she met and married a pastor named Dong Myun Kim. They took the English names of Don and Esther Kim. In the 1950s, they planted Berendo Street Baptist Church in the middle of Koreatown in Los Angeles, where Don pastored for almost 40 years. The couple worked tirelessly together for the gospel for the rest of their lives, doing missionary work and church-planting ministry in South America.

Ei Sook, known in America as Esther Kim, wrote her story in a book called *If I Perish,* one that quickly became the all-time religious bestseller in Korea. It also became a bestseller in Japan and was later turned into a Japanese film. Esther Ahn Kim died in 1997 after facing Alzheimer's. Her nephew, Nathan Kim, wrote about a memory of his favorite aunt, whom he called "Big Mom," a Korean term for an older aunt. He visited her when she was in the late stages of battling her disease:

> I visited her with my father in her small apartment. We sat with her in her living room, and for most of the time I don't think she even realized we were there. She migrated between speaking in English, Korean, and even Japanese frenetically about random things like her students though she hadn't taught school in many decades.

But at one point it seemed she had a moment of clarity. She looked at my father and at me and despaired. She told my father that she felt useless now for God ... that she couldn't even leave her home to tell anyone about Jesus. I was floored that the gospel was so ingrained in this amazing woman that her desire to share the Good News could even break through the grips of such an all-consuming illness like Alzheimer's. I was at a loss for what to tell her. But my father didn't skip a beat.

"No, this is a blessing!" my father interjected, "You used to be so busy, but now you have so much time to pray! You can spend your whole day praying for everyone!"

It was true, and I knew he meant it. So did she. As a look of peace finally came across her face, we took a moment to pray with her and said goodbye. I told her I loved her. It was the last time I saw her. She passed away several months later. Her funeral was attended by VIPs, leaders, and dignitaries. Thousands of people came to pay their respects. Her procession stopped downtown L.A. traffic for miles. But to me she was just my "Big Mom," and I will never know another more faithful woman than her.[18]

Throughout her ministry, Esther Ahn Kim made sure that others knew the source of that faithfulness and endurance, writing, "I knew it would be impossible for me to keep my faith in my own power. God would have to work through me if I was to stand firm."[19]

And in his faithfulness, he did.

LESSONS FROM THE FAITHFUL

What we can learn about steadfast endurance from Esther Ahn Kim

18   Nathan Kim, personal correspondence, November 18, 2019.
19   Esther Ahn Kim, *If I Perish*, 34.

DEPEND ON CHRIST FOR ENDURANCE AND STRENGTH. From the moment of her decision not to bow to the shrine, Esther knew she would need strength from outside herself to endure in faith. She was constantly dependent on Christ for the power to stand firm and walk in obedience. Not only did this awareness drive her to prayerful humility, it also witnessed to others that her strength did not come from her, but from the Holy Spirit.

We are tempted to think we must be strong in order to show others what true faith looks like. But when we do that, we set ourselves up for failure, and we communicate a lie to those around us. Instead, God calls us to depend on him so he gets the glory.

Read 2 Corinthians 4:7–10. What does Paul say is the "treasure" we have in "jars of clay"? What is God's purpose in placing this treasure in weak vessels? Does your life communicate this truth to those around you? In what ways are you trying to be faithful in your own strength?

SEEK TO SHINE AS A LIGHT IN THE DARKNESS. Esther saw the brightness of a few stars against a black sky and was challenged to shine in the same way. She encountered great darkness in Korea, Japan, and in prison, and by the grace of God was able to shine Christ's light to those around her — to guards, fellow prisoners, other Christians, and Japanese officials.

Jesus is the "light of the world" (John 8:12) and calls his followers to be "the light of the world" (Matt. 5:14). Just as he shines in the darkness, he has called us to do the same.

Read Philippians 2:12–16. What does Paul say is the key to shining in the world? How does God's work within his people empower us to shine for his good pleasure? Where has God placed you that is dark and needs light?

EXPECT THAT LOVING OTHERS WILL BE COSTLY AND DIFFICULT. When she heard the moans of the young Chinese woman in the nearby cell, Esther realized she was being called to radically love her. But being called to something doesn't make obedience

31

easy; sometimes it's nearly impossible. As she held the woman's feet against her body for three days, breathing in her horrible stench, Esther was acting in obedience. But as she took those steps of obedience, she realized God was giving her supernatural love for this unlovely young woman.

Similarly, God calls his people to radical love, to obedience in loving others where it might not be reciprocated. We can ask God to give us supernatural love when it is costly and difficult, and that is a prayer he delights to answer.

Read 1 John 4:7–11. How does God show his love to us? These verses make it clear that God loved us before we loved him. How does that encourage you in your difficult relationships?

PREPARE BEFORE THE TRIALS COME. As she was awaiting imprisonment, Esther memorized more than 100 Bible verses and many hymns because she knew a time would come when she would need to have God's Word at the forefront of her mind. In her autobiography, she tells of many moments when Scripture came to mind at just the right time to encourage and strengthen her.

We, too, can prepare for trials during times of peace by steeping in God's Word as a vital source of wisdom and encouragement.

Read Psalm 119:10–11. Why does the psalmist say he has hidden God's Word in his heart? How did this vital spiritual discipline help Esther Ahn Kim during her trials? Write out some passage(s) you want to commit to memory for current trials and future ones.

Sarah Edwards: Steadfast in Service

COURTNEY REISSIG

The year was 1742. Sarah Edwards, a busy pastor's wife and mother, was under considerable stress. Her home was a place of constant activity, nearly always filled with guests and children. Her husband, Jonathan, frequently traveled, and when he was home, he was usually busy studying.

Amid such stress and in the aftermath of the Great Awakening, Sarah encountered her own sort of awakening, one that her friends and acquaintances struggled to classify. In the cold New England winter, she entered a place of darkness and confusion. After spending the morning listening to a man named Buell, who was filling the pulpit while her husband was away, Sarah suddenly fainted upon arrival at home. Shortly after, hallucinations filled her mind, leading to jabbering from her lips. The once strong and steady Sarah seemed to be having a nervous breakdown. She went from being a woman of great efficiency to bedridden, and her friends who were caring for her wondered if Jonathan would come home to find his wife dead, or insane.[1]

In one moment Sarah would be conversing, and in the next she would "lay for a considerable time, faint with joy."[2] Her hallucinations would purge her of anxiety, and then she would faint. This joy mixed with jabbering has led some historians to question the validity of her awakening, but her husband saw it produce good fruit consistent with a true follower of Christ.

Sarah also saw it as life-changing.

. . .

Born as the daughter of a pastor on January 9, 1710, Sarah's world was one of Christian devotion. Her family lived in New Haven, Connecticut, in the parsonage attached to the church. But to be a pastor in Colonial America was unlike today's pastorate. Uncertainty was all around them. Threats of war and attack were ever-present. The land surrounding them, filled with Native Americans, was largely unknown. And the work, without the comfort of modern conveniences, was hard.

Both her mother and father were committed to education and community engagement. Her father was one of the founders of Yale College, and her mother was a descendant of Thomas Hooker, one of the founders of Connecticut.[3] They were set apart as influential and distinguished people. This commitment both to the Lord and also to education created a culture that helped Sarah understand the life of the mind and the soul. It prepared her for marriage to a man — Jonathan Edwards — who would influence religious life for centuries to come.

1   Elizabeth Dodds, *Marriage to a Difficult Man: The Uncommon Union of Jonathan and Sarah Edwards* (Laurel: Audubon Press, 2003), 86.

2   Ibid.

3   Noel Piper, *Faithful Women and Their Extraordinary God* (Wheaton: Crossway Books, 2005), 15.

Jonathan was a man beyond his time. He began college at age 13, and by the age of 19, he had already graduated and been pastoring for a year.[4] Unlike Sarah, he did not possess eloquent social skills. His intellect was outsized, which led him to spend his life in books and writing. In contrast, Sarah was able to connect spiritual devotion with hospitality. Her training as a member of polite New England society, along with her devotion to the Lord, enabled Sarah to create a welcoming home environment for people to be ministered to by her husband's intellect and spiritual insight. Without her social prowess, Jonathan would not have been able to influence such a wide range of people.

Sarah was so shaped by the ministry of her father's preaching and life in a Christian home that when she was only 13, Jonathan noticed her devotion to the Lord:

They saw there is a young lady in New Haven who is beloved of the Great Being who made and rules the world, and that there are certain seasons in which this Great Being, in some way or other invisible, comes to her and fills her mind with exceeding sweet delight, and that she hardly cares for anything except to meditate on Him; that she expects after a while to be received up where He is, to be raised out of the world and caught up into heaven, being assured that He loves her too well to let her remain at a distance from Him always ... She is of a wonderful sweetness, calmness, and universal benevolence of mind, especially after this Great God has manifested Himself to her mind. She will sometimes go about from place to place, singing sweetly; and seems to be always full of joy and pleasure, and no one knows for what. She loves to be alone, walking in the field

4   Ibid., 16.

and groves, and seems to have someone invisible always conversing with her.[5]

Sarah combined doctrinal fidelity with a deep faith that elicited emotion. Jonathan was drawn to her devotion to the Lord, and they were married on July 28, 1727, when she was 17 and he was 24. Communion with God was a daily necessity for both Jonathan and Sarah. It prepared her for her own spiritual awakening — and the difficult days to come.

PREPARATION FOR DIFFICULT DAYS

Early in her marriage, Sarah quickly grew busy, which intensified her need to remain utterly dependent on the Lord for his constant presence and strength. Because of the nature of Jonathan's work and disposition, much of the housework fell to her. Plagued by perpetual physical ailments, Jonathan kept to a strict diet to conserve his energy for studying and writing. He woke early in the morning to work, and would only emerge for occasional meals and time with family. He spent nearly 12 hours a day studying and would often take his meals in his study. Jonathan's work was so intense that he bore "uncertainties in thought and theology as if they were physical stress."[6] He was firm in his convictions and would refuse to budge once he came to them. To be married to such an intelligent, enlightened man

---

5   Jennifer Adams, *In Love With Christ: The Narrative of Sarah Edwards* (Forest: Corner Pillar Press, 2010), 19.
6   Piper, *Faithful Women and Their Extraordinary God*, 18.

was to be constantly reminded of his otherworldliness, and aware of imminent threats of conflict.

Many know of Jonathan Edwards because of his prolific pen and influence in the First Great Awakening. This time of spiritual revival was pervasive across the 13 colonies, affecting them for years to come. But during this time Jonathan was also frequently called away to preach. On top of the stress of his absence, the Edwards family faced financial difficulty as their family grew in number and need. Jonathan asked the parish for a set salary, but his request was not taken favorably. So, while he was away preaching, Sarah was tasked with itemizing every purchase for the parish in order to protect them from extravagant living.

Sarah also was perpetually pregnant, having a baby nearly every two years, totaling 11 children. On top of the physical needs of caring for small children (while also recovering from birth or laid low by pregnancy) there were other daily needs:

> Breaking ice to haul water, bringing in firewood and tending the fire, cooking and packing lunches for visiting travelers, making the family's clothing (from sheep-shearing through spinning and weaving to sewing), growing and preserving produce, making brooms, doing laundry, tending babies and nursing illnesses, making candles, feeding poultry, overseeing butchering, teaching the boys whatever they didn't learn at school, and seeing that the girls learned homemaking creativity. And that was only a fraction of Sarah's responsibilities, houseguests who required her hospitality and care, and the discipline and instruction of children.[7]

The woman who spent her younger years seeking closeness to the Lord was also a young mother who spent her exhausting days in the same pursuit. Sarah's service was never-ending, but she did it with

7   Ibid., 23.

joy. God's sanctifying work in her heart was his means of teaching her to do "whatever her hand finds her to do with all her might" (Eccles. 9:10). "Oh how good," she said, "it is to work for God in the day-time and at night to lie down under His smiles."[8]

Sarah handled her tasks with grace and kindness. Those who entered her home found it a welcome respite to their travels. Later, her children would reflect on her patience and grace toward them, and her husband delighted in her. He remembered her contentedness in her work: "She said that when she carried out her daily responsibilities as unto the Lord, they were found to be as good as prayer."[9]

We all have work to do that can hardly feel "as good as prayer." For Sarah, her faithfulness in her daily work was directly owing to her contented spirit under the Lord's direction in her life. God had captured her heart through the preaching of the Word, the discipline of Scripture reading, and the practice of prayer. She could face the challenges of colonial America and ministry because God was at work.

WOMAN AT BEST

Amid all of Sarah's strengths, she had shortcomings and blind spots. Like many others in their community, the Edwards family owned slaves. While they were known for loving and caring for their slaves, their misguided ideology behind slavery was still apparent to Sarah:

> Sarah Edwards had this same firm, quiet manner with her own domestic help. She treated her slaves with appreciation but with dignity. She maintained a distance between them as she felt befitted the scriptural order, the difference between servant and master. She felt, however, that all men, although different

8   Adams, *In Love With Christ*, 100.
9   Ibid.

in station, were equal in the sight of God; but her upbringing made it difficult to practice this Christian principle. She confessed she had trouble regarding a slave as her equal in the sight of God. She was troubled by her disobedience to God's clear teaching on this matter, and, after much wrestling with her conscience, she finally reached, she announced, that state of grace where she would not only permit but would be happy to let a negro slave precede her into heaven. Her slaves were tenderly cared for and loved, but they sat in the slave gallery in church and did not sit with the family.[10]

It's easy to read this account and be appalled, especially given the distance from slavery in America. It would also be easy to dismiss Sarah Edwards as a bigot unworthy of admiration and dismiss her broader influence and witness to Christ. Yet many revered Christian heroes engaged in and approved of practices that the Bible calls sinful. We can learn from them while also grieving their failures. Slavery was a large blind spot for Sarah, and for many others in colonial America. Her humane treatment of her slave, Venus, while commendable, does not remove the fact that her ideology that led to owning slaves is offensive in the sight of God.

HER GREAT AWAKENING

Sarah's early years of marriage were the foundation for the awakening that came in January 1742. Weighed down by her sin, depleted

---

10   Edna Gerstner, *Jonathan and Sarah: An Uncommon Union* (Morgan: Soli Deo Gloria Publications, 1995), 156.

by years of childbearing, and most likely exhausted from the difficult labor of life, God met Sarah in an extraordinary way. She wrote,

> God the Father, and the Lord Jesus Christ, seemed as distinct persons both manifesting their inconceivable loveliness, mildness, and gentleness, and their great immutable love to me. My *mind* was so deeply impressed with the love of Christ and a sense of His immediate presence that I could with difficulty refrain from rising from my seat and leaping for joy.[11]

Prior to this event, Sarah had been weighed down by besetting sins, most notably her jealousy for her husband's advancement and an intense fear of man (which makes sense because she was under such scrutiny). Her commitment to Jonathan as a devoted wife was admirable, but it led to envy of those who were perceived to be more successful than him.[12] During this two-week revival, this sin was rooted out. And it was evident to all who knew her.

There is no doubt that, afterward, Sarah Edwards emerged a changed and liberated person. It was a week of emotional crisis — but in its aftermath was a new life, grounded on practical, spiritual reality and accompanied by many other challenges, the sharpest of which came in 1745.[13]

HEAVY GRIEF OF LOSS

David Brainerd, the great missionary to the Native Americans, stayed with the Edwards family in 1745 while he was suffering from what would eventually be named tuberculosis. Jonathan and Sarah's daughter, Jerusha, nursed him throughout his illness until he even-

11 Adams, *In Love With Christ*, 52.
12 Gerstner, *Jonathan and Sarah*, 158.
13 Dodds, *Marriage to a Difficult Man*, 86.

tually succumbed in October. At the time, no one knew the virility of tuberculosis, and 19 weeks after Brainerd's death, Jerusha died as well.

Until this point, Sarah had avoided the death of a child, which was largely unheard of in colonial America. Death was all around her, so she was not surprised by it; but it did come as a hard blow. Two months after the death of Jerusha, Sarah gave birth to Elizabeth, who ended up with rickets. Jerusha's death had affected her entire being, which led to this birth complication. As one biographer notes, the death of Sarah's daughter was a "scar she would carry forever."[14]

To add to the grief of losing Jerusha and having a frail child to care for, Jonathan came up against a significant struggle in his parish in Northampton over theological matters. He was forced to stand alone and ultimately was fired from his position. This led the Edwards family to move to the Stockbridge, where the Native Americans needed a pastor. Here they faced new challenges, but also found great opportunities for their children, as well as for Jonathan to think and write.

FAMILY BEREAVED

Jonathan and Sarah's daughter, Esther, eventually married Aaron Burr Sr.[15] who died unexpectedly, leaving Esther a widow and the College of New Jersey (where he was president) without a leader. Jonathan was approached about taking over, so he traveled to New Jersey for the position. While there, he agreed to take part in an experimental smallpox inoculation, as did Esther and her children. Smallpox was deadly, virulent, and rampant in New Jersey, so it

---

14   Ibid., 110.
15   They became the parents of the future Vice President of the United States, Aaron Burr, Jr.

seemed like a necessary step to protect the family. It had the opposite effect, and Jonathan succumbed to the disease on March 22, 1758. A little more than two weeks later, Esther died as well.

The blow to the Edwards family was significant. The trip to New Jersey was supposed to be one of fruitfulness for Jonathan and his work. Instead, it stole from the Edwards family a husband and father and orphaned Esther's two children.

Sarah did what any grandmother would do, and she went to retrieve the children. There was no question that she would care for them and serve them. But even this plan was cut short. Sarah Edwards contracted dysentery on the trip home and died on October 2, 1758, with none of her family by her side.

While Jonathan and Sarah did not live to see their descendants grow up, their legacy lives on. Their grandchildren and great-grandchildren affected American culture, the church, even the whole world. They became politicians, college presidents, pastors, and faithful church members. Sarah did not live to see her 50th birthday, but her influence long outlived her.

LESSONS FROM THE FAITHFUL

What we can learn about steadfast endurance from Sarah Edwards

GLADLY SUBMIT TO GOD'S PRUNING WORK. Sarah's great awakening changed her on a number of fronts. Her transformed life was so intense that Jonathan found a number of reasons to commend her: Her work carried new purpose. Her desire to live for Christ was strengthened. Her assurance of salvation was solidified. She walked forward from this encounter with confidence not in herself, but in God.

God transformed her in one particular area that many of us can relate to: the temptation toward comparison and envy. Sarah often compared herself to others, her husband's work to the work of others, and even her own spiritual progress to that of others. She spent a great deal of time weighed down by her sin and weakness. But God used Sarah's awakening to transform her into Christlikeness. We may not have a two-week period of unprecedented encounters with the living God, but we can relate to God's pruning work as he makes us more like Christ by cutting out the sin that entangles us.

Read John 15:1–2. What does Jesus say is the Father's purpose in his pruning work? How has God pruned you, and how have you seen him use that pruning to make you bear more fruit? This might be fruit of repentance, giftings, holiness, or other fruit of the Spirit.

LEARN THE SECRET OF CONTENTMENT IN ALL CIRCUM-STANCES. Sarah's confidence in God would prove to be a sustaining grace in trials. Perhaps God allowed her to see him in greater measure during her awakening to provide her with the comforting strength of his presence in her deepest valleys of loss and sorrow. Either way, the encounter marked her and prepared her for contentment in seasons of service and suffering.

Read Philippians 4:11–13. According to Paul, what is contentment? What does he say is "the secret" to facing any circumstance with such contentment? In what areas do you need to learn contentment?

PURSUE FAITHFUL SERVICE IN THE ORDINARY. Sarah's life, though remarkable in a number of ways, was ordinary. In fact, her commitment to regular rhythms prepared her for the remarkable encounter with God that brought forth so much fruit. Her ordinary faithfulness in the mundane moments is a great teacher.

While the ways Sarah served might look different than ours, they were just as ordinary. Children still need love, attention, and instruction. Hungry bellies need to be filled. Laundry needs to be done. The tools for accomplishing those tasks might change with time, but we are still called to pursue faithful service in ordinary, repetitive tasks. Lest we think we cannot be as spiritually devoted as the wife of the great Jonathan Edwards, it's helpful to remember that her spiritual devotion was grown over a lifetime of small deposits of service.

Even if we never have such a miraculous encounter with God like Sarah did, we are called to pursue ordinary acts of faithfulness. As we make these small deposits of spiritual disciplines, we will increasingly bear good fruit, learn repentance, and develop a greater trust in the Lord.

Read 1 Corinthians 15:58. What four actions does Scripture call us to, even in the most ordinary work? How can your work, whatever that is, be done "in the Lord"? How does Sarah's faithfulness in the ordinariness of her work encourage you toward faithfulness in your own?

Elisabeth Elliot: Steadfast in Loss

ABIGAIL DODDS

"Mama, who *is* that? Is that my daddy?"[1]

A small child named Valerie Elliot asked this direct and honest question. Valerie had come with her mother, Elisabeth Elliot, to live in a remote jungle among a people responsible for the murder of her father.

Elisabeth explains in a letter written from the Ecuadorian jungle,

> ... the first day we arrived, Val just sat down on the log which Kimu was squatting on and stared and stared. Then she said, 'Mama, who IS that? Is that my daddy? He looks like a daddy.' Somehow, in her child mind, she had associated Aucas and daddy — though I never told her till a few days ago that the Aucas had killed her daddy. I waited till she had met five of the

1   Letter to Marj Saint and Marilou McCully. Billy Graham Center Archives: Collection 278, Box 4, Folder 6, https://www2.wheaton.edu/bgc/archives/docs/eelliotletter/003.htm.

men and then I told her that those men had killed daddy. She said, "Oh." She prays for them and for the others she knows by name.[2]

With her usual candor and simplicity, Elisabeth gave her daughter a gift that so many long to be given by their mother: the gift of the truth. Her words could be relied upon to not only tell the truth, but to do so with clarity — which is at least partly why Elisabeth Elliot has become a spiritual mother to so many women, both young and old. Her unvarnished and direct speech has been like a life preserver named Reality, thrown to those adrift. She's helped many find the solid ground of Christ when fluidity and relativism have threatened to drown them.

In the words of her dear friend Joni Eareckson Tada, "Elisabeth Elliot was the saltiest of the salt of the earth."[3]

. . .

Born in Belgium to missionary parents on December 21, 1926, Elisabeth Howard would not be in Belgium for long. Her father, Philip E. Howard Jr., accepted a position with *The Sunday School Times*, and they moved to the United States, settling in Philadelphia, Pennsylvania, when she was only 5 months old. She was the second child and first daughter of what would eventually be six Howard children.

Raised in a disciplined and well-ordered home, Elisabeth (called Betty by her family and close friends) grew up with daily rhythms of Bible reading, prayer, and hymn-singing. She also grew

2   Letter to Marj Saint and Marilou McCully.
3   "Elisabeth Elliot Memorial Service at Wheaton College." Filmed July 31, 2015. https://www.youtube.com/watch?v=WSi3mR9GQIE.

up with "books in every room ... we were surrounded by books."[4] These were not the great literary works of the day, but rather books from authors like Matthew Henry, Charles Spurgeon, and Jonathan Edwards. Her father also kept a dictionary near the dining room table, so that proper pronunciation and meaning of unknown words could be looked up as needed by his children.[5] For all the structure and learning, however, the Howard home was full of good humor: "My father had a very dry sense of humor and [was] very self-deprecating and we would just die laughing at his descriptions of himself. I can see my mother wiping her eyes at the table laughing at my father."[6]

Elisabeth didn't know the exact date on which she trusted in Christ for salvation. But at age ten, she recalled hearing Irwin Moon relay John 3:3, "You must be born again." Then she made a public profession of faith in Jesus Christ, even though she had always considered herself a Christian. At 12, she submitted herself to Jesus as Lord and prayed, "Lord, I want you to do anything you want with me."[7]

When Elisabeth was 14, she first encountered the writing of Amy Carmichael, the Irish missionary to India, whose poems she delighted in and memorized. Outside of Elisabeth's parents, Amy Carmichael was her greatest spiritual influence. She would go on to write Carmichael's biography, *A Chance to Die: The Life and Legacy of Amy Carmichael*. Carmichael's utter devotion to the Lord and complete obedience to his will captured Elisabeth's imagina-

4   Elisabeth Elliot, "Interview of Elisabeth Howard Gren by Robert Shuster," interview by Robert Shuster, March 26, 1985, audio, Billy Graham Center Archives: Collection 278, Tape T2, https://web.archive.org/web/20160305211246/http://www2.wheaton.edu/bgc/archives/trans/278t02.htm.
5   Elliot, interview.
6   Elliot, interview.
7   Elliot, interview.

tion. She often quoted Carmichael's words, "In acceptance lieth peace" — words that had made a home on her lips and in her heart.

LOVE DEFERRED, LOVE ADORNED

Elisabeth began her college career at Wheaton College in 1944 toward the end of World War II. There, the call to foreign missions was confirmed in her, and she began to study classical Greek in hope that it would serve in future Bible translation.

At Wheaton she met Jim Elliot. Jim was, in Elisabeth's words, "a big man on campus," which was a far cry from how she described herself: "a wallflower."[8] Yet these two intensely passionate and single-minded young people were drawn to each other in a similarly intense and passionate way.

Both Jim and Elisabeth were headed for the mission field. Both sensed a call to Ecuador. But Jim would need more assurance that marrying Elisabeth would not be a distraction to his mission, but part and parcel of it. While each waited for God's guidance in their relationship, God was teaching Elisabeth a posture that she would return to her whole life long — one of surrender, of bent knees and open hands.

Thankfully, their love would not be deferred forever. In 1953, Jim and Elisabeth were married in Quito, Ecuador. She wore a sky-blue dress suit, and a handful of friends witnessed the event. They chose this verse from Isaiah for their wedding: "Lo, this is our God; we have waited for him."[9]

They continued their missionary work among the Quichua Indians of Ecuador. In February 1955, Elisabeth gave birth to their daughter, Valerie. Their long-deferred love was now adorned with a

8   Valerie Elliot Shepard, *Devotedly: The Personal Letters and Love Story of Jim and Elisabeth Elliot* (Nashville: B&H Publishing Group, 2019), 3.
9   Ibid., 274.

beautiful baby girl. They enjoyed ten months together as husband, wife, and child.

DEVOTION AMID LOSS

Not three years after their marriage, Jim Elliot, along with four other missionary men, set out to make contact with tribal people known as the Waorani (formerly called the Aucas). The men knew that previous attempts to enter the tribe had ended with death. Their goal was to establish friendly contact, and they wished to take the good news to a people and a place where it had never been taken before. In 1955, they made drops of gifts from an airplane to the beach where the Waorani lived and simultaneously broadcasted what they knew of the Waorani language from the plane. On January 6, 1956, all seemed to be going as hoped. So they landed and made contact with some members of the tribe, even giving one of them a ride on their airplane.

But two days later, on January 8, 1956, a group of men from the tribe unexpectedly speared the five men to death on the beach. After days of no radio contact, a United States Air Force helicopter crew landed at the site of the massacre and found all five bodies. They buried them where they fell.[10]

Meanwhile, five young wives were receiving shortwave radio communication from Seattle, Washington, to Quito, Ecuador, where they were waiting for word of their husbands. Kenneth Fleming, the

10   Summary of conversations Kenneth Flemming had with Olive Fleming, Elisabeth Elliot, Marilou McCully, Marj Saint, and Barbara Youderian while they were at Shell Mera. Billy Graham Center Archives, Collection 657, Box 2, Folder 11. https://www2.wheaton.edu/bgc/archives/exhibits/Ecuador1956/03%20Event%2009.htm. One of the bodies was identified before being washed away in the river. https://www.thegospelcoalition.org/blogs/justin-taylor/they-were-no-fools-60-years-ago-today-the-martyrdom-of-jim-elliot-and-four-other-missionaries/.

father of Pete Fleming (one of the men who was murdered), was able to communicate with the women on January 12, 1953. Here is his assessment of those fresh young widows:

1. That during the entire duration of their ordeal, all five young wives were together at Shell Mera.
2. That all were bearing up in unbelievable fashion.
3. That during the period of uncertainty as to the fate of the fifth member of the party the girls decided that they did not wish to be told the identities of those who had been found and of that one still missing.
4. That all five are content in the knowledge that God, who knows the end from the beginning can make no mistake, and that their present position is the result of either His directive or permissive will.
5. That in joint conference they had decided that it would be un-necessary for anyone to come from the U.S. to assist them.
6. That they were in constant prayer that the Lord would direct their future movements, and that they were unwilling to make any decisions or take any steps until they were SURE that such would be in conformity with the will of God.[11]

Fleming's report will not surprise anyone who has read anything of Elisabeth Elliot's writing. "Bearing up," "constant prayer," and "conformity with the will of God" are exactly what she is known for to her readers. However, at that point Elisabeth Elliot wasn't *known* to anyone outside her family and close friends. She was an obscure woman who had not yet published a book. But she had penned her very soul on the pages of her journal in prayer to the Lord. Her letters to Jim over the course of their six-year relationship coursed

11 Summary of conversations Kenneth Flemming had with Olive Fleming, Elis-abeth Elliot, Marilou McCully, Marj Saint, and Barbara Youderian while they were at Shell Mera.

with the pure and unassuming thoughts of a woman whose brilliance paired with complete devotion to God — a reality that made her brilliance even brighter, in God's matchless ways.

Elisabeth Elliot's response to her husband's murder was not calculated to suit an audience; it was not filtered to meet anyone's expectations. It was the response of a woman wholly dependent on God. And it was this obscure and unassuming woman, living in the jungle of Ecuador, on whom God would shine a spotlight for all the world to see.

'EVERYTHING IN LIFE'

This young mother would soon find herself on the pages of *Time* magazine, in a full photo spread of herself and her daughter among the same people who murdered her husband. Yes, Elisabeth Elliot stayed in Ecuador after her husband's body had been put in the ground there. She continued the work with the Quichua Indians for two years. Then, on October 8, 1958, after limited study of the Waorani language and prayerful planning, she began to make her home with the Waorani people, along with her daughter, Val, and Rachel Saint.

She wrote in a letter to Marj Saint and Marilou McCully (two of her fellow widows),

> But I have now met four of the seven men who killed our husbands. It is a very strange thing thus to find oneself between two very remote sides of a story. To us, it meant everything in life and continues to mean that. To these simple, laughing, carefree forest people, killing five men was little more than routine and they had probably nearly forgotten about it.[12]

12   Letter to Marj Saint and Marilou McCully.

She entered the world of the Waorani and discovered how the event that had irretrievably altered her life had had little to no effect on them. They had taken from her "everything in life." Yet her response was not bitterness or anger. It was not self-pity. Instead, she chose love and good humor, writing in the same letter to Marj and Marilou, "I wish you could hear the singing at night!" She continued,

> The Auca men sit with solemn gaze, hands clasped in front of chest, and chant in three parts — a single minor chord, unvaried through literally hundreds of repetitions of a seven-beat phrase. It is fantastically hypnotic. I made a tape recording of it. (This business of trying to record 1) in a diary, 2) in letters, 3) in photographs, and 4) on tape — besides trying to take down language data and keep Val amused, can get complicated. To say nothing of the 9-step cup of coffee!)[13]

Her good humor hums in every sentence, her smile lurking behind the words, making light what was undoubtedly heavy. This, too, was a gift of God's remarkable grace. Her brother and daughter tell of her irrepressible mimicry, how she regaled her family with her impeccable accents, some of which made their way into her public speaking.

In 1960, Elisabeth and Valerie came to America. One year later, in 1961, they returned to Ecuador, but soon left the Waorani tribe to continue work with the Quichua Indians. Finally, in 1963, they moved to Franconia, New Hampshire, where Elisabeth continued her public speaking and writing, which began as a result of her first book, *Through Gates of Splendor* (1957), the story of the five missionary men whose lives ended so suddenly. But this transition away from the peoples of Ecuador was not without sorrow:

13   Letter to Marj Saint and Marilou McCully.

At the end of my eleven years in that country, my labors seemed to have turned to ashes. One set of translation notes was in a suitcase that was stolen from the top of a banana truck. My Auca materials sit in my attic to this day. Only a portion of my Quichua work was useful to two other missionaries.[14]

Yet, in returning home, she continued to fulfill Jim's parting words to her. Before his departure to make contact with the Waorani, they discussed the possibility that he may not return. His charge to her was, "Teach the believers, darling. We've got to teach the believers."[15]

FRUITFUL IN EVERY SEASON

Elisabeth's writings have been teaching believers ever since. But her teaching has been a letter written by the constancy of her life, not only by the truthfulness of her words.

In 1969, Elisabeth married Addison Leitch, a professor at Tarkio College. Later, they moved to Massachusetts, where he became professor of theology at Gordon-Conwell Theological Seminary. She also joined the faculty at Gordon-Conwell as an adjunct professor after Addison died of cancer in 1973.

On December 21, 1977, Elisabeth married Lars Gren. They would remain together until her death. Gren eventually became her agent, representing Elisabeth and her many popular books, such as *Shadow of the Almighty*, *These Strange Ashes*, *Let Me Be a Woman*, *Passion and Purity*, *Discipline: The Glad Surrender*, and *A Path Through Suffering*. In October 1988 she began a daily radio program

---

14   Elisabeth Elliot, "Farewells," *The Elisabeth Elliot Newsletter* (November/December 2003), http://www.elisabethelliot.org/newsletters/2003-11-12.pdf.

15   "Elisabeth Elliot Memorial Service at Wheaton College." Quotation shared by Valerie Shepard.

called *Gateway to Joy*. Her words reverberated through countless hearts: "You are loved with an everlasting love." This radio program continued until 2001, and two years after that, in 2003, her newsletter also came to an end. In it, she recounts how the loss of her linguistic notebooks turned her years of labor into ashes.[16] This was a strange fruitfulness, indeed.

Elisabeth was a stalwart, but she was no stoic. She did not merely grin and bear it in trials; rather she placed her hand in her Savior's and determined that where he led, she would follow. How could she know how many would be following after her, eagerly reaching for the hand of God that held her so secure?

In that final newsletter she goes on to confront the deaths of Jim and Addison that left her twice bereft. She concludes with Addison's words, spoken before his death: "One cannot unscrew the Inscrutable." She continues, "God's ways are mysterious and our faith develops strong muscles as we negotiate the twists and turns of our lives."

Elisabeth mothered only one child. According to worldly judgments, when it comes to biological fruitfulness, one might think her sparse. However, not only did her daughter give her eight grandchildren, but also Elisabeth became a spiritual mother to more than we will know in this life. It's hard not to think of God telling Abraham to behold the stars in the sky, saying, "So shall your offspring be" (Gen. 15:5). In Christ, Elisabeth was fruitful beyond reckoning.

NO EMPTY WORD

God used Elisabeth Elliot's spiritual mothering to do more than comfort the suffering. He also used her to give a generation of Christian women spines of self-pity-hating steel. C. S. Lewis said, "Cour-

---

16   Elliot, "Farewells."

age is not simply one of the virtues but the form of every virtue at the testing point, which means at the point of highest reality."

Elisabeth committed to be and do exactly what God had made her to be and do, which not only applied to her missionary calling; it also applied to her calling as a woman. It was her courage in the places where courage was required that set her apart. When the culture and church were largely stepping outside God's design for women, she did not shrink, but once again set an example. She put it this way:

> I don't want anybody treating me as a 'person' rather than as a woman. Our sexual differences are the terms of our life, and to obscure them in any way is to weaken the very fabric of life itself. Some women fondly imagine a new beginning of liberty, but it is in reality a new bondage, more bitter than anything they seek to be liberated from.[17]

Elisabeth would suffer no liberty that was not to be found in her Lord and Master. And she boldly called for other women to follow suit through her chapter in *Recovering Biblical Manhood and Womanhood*. Despite her many popular books, this message was not universally loved and accepted, even among Christians. Her words are heavy on the page with prophetic wisdom — but prophets are not known for their popular appeal. Yet this was no deterrent for the woman whose surrender to God had led her to know, love, and be a witness of Christ to her husband's murderers.

She did not play games — not with God, and not with those to whom she wrote her books or spoke on public radio or counseled in private. Elisabeth did not speak empty words. She told the truth exactly as she received it — straight from his Book without compro-

17   Elisabeth Elliot, *Let Me Be a Woman: Notes to my Daughter on the Meaning of Womanhood* (Wheaton: Tyndale House Publishers, 1976), 93.

mise and without sugar-coating, whether it be about suffering, womanhood, or the utter obedience to which God calls us in his Son.

IN PURSUIT OF HOLINESS

Some may think her ways too high or holy or unattainable for common folk. But Elisabeth knew her own need — her weaknesses, failures, even her sinfulness. She wrote in her journal, "Oh Lord help me, for I am truly helpless."[18] Undergirding all the confidence and security that she found in the Lord was the clear-eyed and never-changing reality that, apart from him, she was truly helpless. She did not stand on a foundation of her own efforts, but on the foundation of her Perfect King and Treasure.

"Heaven is a place for holy inhabitants and Elisabeth got herself ready for heaven by making holiness her entire life's pursuit and passion." Joni Eareckson Tada made this assessment at Elisabeth's memorial service after her death on June 15, 2015. Elisabeth was 88 years old. She endured ten years of dementia before the Lord took her home.

In a time where spiritual diets consist primarily of sentimental sweets, Elisabeth's life and words savored strongly of the flint-faced Christ. She was "the saltiest of the salt of the earth," and the saltiness of her life has preserved and kept many for Christ. She bid farewell in her newsletter with a hymn by Anna L. Waring containing this line that aptly describes Elisabeth Elliot's legacy: "In service which thy will appoints, there are no bonds for me . . . a life of self-renouncing love is one of liberty."[19]

18   "Elisabeth Elliot Memorial Service at Wheaton College."
19   Elliot, "Farewells."

LESSONS FROM THE FAITHFUL

What we can learn about steadfast endurance from Elisabeth Elliot

CONSIDER HOW YOU MEASURE FRUITFULNESS. Biological fruitfulness is a good gift of God to be celebrated, but it is not the only fruitfulness we should consider. Elisabeth mothered many women, despite having only one biological child. She also bore the fruit of the Spirit, perhaps most notably the fruit of self-control — a struggle for many of us.

Read Galatians 5:16–26 and Titus 2:3–5. How can you reorient your thinking to consider fruitfulness in spiritual ways? How might God be wanting to increase your fruitfulness in his kingdom? Is there a particular fruit of the Spirit lacking in your life?

SURRENDER EVERYTHING TO GOD — HOLD NOTHING BACK. At the age of 12, Elisabeth prayed, "Lord, I want you to do anything you want with me." During her painstaking courtship with Jim, while laboring among indigenous tribes, and through various trials, Elisabeth's heart was in a posture of submission to the Lord's hand and plan. She counted his thoughts and words as more precious than her own and considered what he gave her as better than what she would have chosen for herself. Her life pulsed with the Christly prayer, "Not my will, but yours be done."

Read Romans 12:1–2. What does Paul say is the essence of spiritual worship? What motivates our worship? Consider what is holding you back from offering yourself wholly to God, and pray that he would keep you from conforming to the world, but would transform your mind so that you would be able to discern his perfect will and surrender to him in everything.

SPEAK THE TRUTH IN LOVE. Since Elisabeth was so committed to the truth of God, some might wrongly assume that she went around recklessly stomping on people's feelings. But if Elisabeth stomped on anything, it was sinful feelings run amok. Elisabeth understood how untrustworthy our feelings can be, so she took care to subject hers to God's Word. She spoke the truth, and she did so from a heart of love — first and foremost out of love for God, then love for others — which is different from running roughshod over people out of a need to air one's thoughts.

Read Ephesians 4:11–16. Why is it important for us to speak the truth in love to one another? What steps can you take to grow in this area?

Corrie ten Boom: Steadfast in Darkness

CHRISTINE HOOVER

Between rows of beds in a dark, rancid bunkhouse, Corrie ten Boom trudged behind her prison guard, searching for an empty bunk where she and her sister, Betsie, could rest their weary bodies. The beds were square platforms stacked three high and wedged in every possible area of the bunkhouse, an enormous dormitory of sorts for women. This, however, was not a dormitory; it was a glorified prison cell in Ravensbruck, a concentration camp located deep in the cold, dark heart of Nazi Germany.

The guard stopped and pointed to an unclaimed spot on a second-tier bunk, so close to the one above it that neither sister would be able to sit up without bumping her head. As Corrie and Betsie climbed into the bunk, they were met with the nauseating smell of soiled straw along with the startling realization that the straw was flea-infested. The fleas set upon them immediately, causing Corrie

59

to jump out of the bunk, scratching and flailing, as she cried out to her sister, "Betsie, how can we live in such a place?"[1]

Betsie's answer was more startling to Corrie than the fleas. She recalled what the sisters had read together earlier that morning in their contraband Bible: "Rejoice always, pray constantly, give thanks in all circumstances; for this is the will of God in Christ Jesus" (1 Thess. 5:16–18). Betsie's startling answer was that they should obey Scripture by giving thanks to God for every single thing in their barracks: for their shared bunk, their contraband Bible, even the crowded beds that meant more female prisoners would hear that very Bible's words of life. Without hesitation, Betsie began to pray, ticking off all her surroundings — until, finally, she finished her prayer with, "And thank you, God, for the fleas."

The fleas! This was too much for Corrie, and she said so with indignation: "Betsie, there's no way even God can make me grateful for a flea."[2] Though Corrie was incredulous, uncertain how the light of Christ could shine in such a dark place, she'd soon watch him do exactly what she most doubted he could do.

She'd soon thank God for the fleas.

. . .

Corrie couldn't yet see it, but throughout her life God had been preparing her for Ravensbruck, implanting truths from his Word and lessons from her parents that would feed her again and again in a place of thirst and starvation.

Corrie was born in Holland in 1892 to a devout Christian couple, Casper and Cornelia ten Boom. They lived in old Haarlem in what the Dutch called a Beje, a tall and narrow house, which the ten Booms had cordoned off into various rooms for Corrie's aunts

---

1   Corrie ten Boom, Elizabeth Sherrill, and John Sherrill, *The Hiding Place* (Grand Rapids: Chosen Books, 2006), location 3575. Kindle.
2   Ibid., location 3599.

and siblings. The family business — a watch shop — was attached
to the bottom floor of their home. Later, as a young woman in her
20s, Corrie would learn the business from her father and would
eventually become the first licensed female watchmaker in Holland,
building and repairing timepieces for more than 20 years in the ten
Boom's shop.

Corrie's family enjoyed high esteem in Haarlem. Her father,
much beloved by his customers, welcomed 11 foster children into his
family after Corrie and her three siblings were grown. Her mother
(who died when Corrie was 27) consistently met the needs of the
poor in the city and, after becoming an invalid, served others faithfully through prayer.

Casper and Cornelia passed their faith in Christ to their four
children, not just in deed but also in word. Each morning at 8:30
a.m. the family and shop employees gathered at the breakfast table
for Bible reading and prayer. One morning, Corrie's father read
from Psalm 119: "Thy word is a lamp unto my feet, and a light unto
my path ... Thou art my hiding place and my shield. I hope in thy
word." Corrie couldn't stop wondering why God was called a hiding
place. Her world was happy and light. What could she possibly need
to hide from?

Corrie's parents took every opportunity to help her apply the
Scriptures they read aloud each morning. When Corrie was a young
child, she accompanied her mother to the home of a woman whose
baby had died the previous night. Upon arrival, her mother went at
once to the grieving woman, but Corrie stood, frozen, at the thresh-
old. The intangible idea of death had suddenly become too real, and
Corrie's heart filled with terror. That night, as her father tucked her
into bed, he addressed her fear of losing her loved ones.

"Corrie," he began gently, "when you and I go to Amster-
dam — when do I give you your ticket?"

[Corrie] sniffed a few times, considering this.

"Why, just before we get on the train."

"Exactly. And our wise Father in heaven knows when we're going to need things, too. Don't run out ahead of Him, Corrie. When the time comes that some of us will have to die, you will look into your heart and find the strength you need — just in time."[3]

RUMBLINGS OF DARKNESS

When the ten Boom siblings grew up, her sister, Nollie, and her brother, Willem, both got married and started families of their own. Betsie, the oldest, and Corrie, the youngest, continued living at home with their widowed father. Betsie cared for the home and the many people who came in and out of the Beje. Corrie worked in the shop, tending the books and making and repairing watches. In her early 20s, she fell deeply in love with a man named Karel; but the young man's parents expected him to marry above Corrie's station, and so the relationship painfully dissolved. In fact, as she looked on happily at Nollie's wedding, she knew she would never marry. Yet she prayed for the well-being of the man she had loved and even for his new bride, knowing the Lord had aided her in her ability to pray for them.

Though the Beje continued to be a warm, happy place, outside its doors were rumblings of trouble. Back in 1927, Corrie's brother Willem had returned to Holland from pursuing his doctoral thesis in Germany and warned of looming problems. The Nazi Party, he said, was systematically teaching disrespect for the old and the weak, even proposing their elimination. Willem became a pastor, heading the Dutch Reformed Church's outreach to Jews. By the late 1930s, he had opened a home for displaced Jews who were coming in droves from Germany with horrifying tales of Nazi oppression.

3   Ibid., location 640–647.

Rumors of war threatened Holland in those years. But Holland's prime minister assured his countrymen that they would avoid war by remaining neutral and, therefore, they had nothing to fear. Casper ten Boom, hearing the prime minister's speech over radio broadcast, turned to his daughters and said, "It is wrong to give people hope when there is no hope ... there will be war. The Germans will attack and we will fall."[4] Five hours after the prime minister's speech, during the early hours of May 10, 1940, the Germans attacked neutral Holland, taking only five days to force its surrender and occupy the country.

During the occupation, as Corrie left the Beje for business or her daily walks, she began noting small and confounding changes around her: stars of David appearing on passersby, windows of Jewish businesses shattered by rocks, signs barring Jews from public spaces, and ugly words defaming synagogue walls. To Corrie, these seemed to be a test: how many Dutchmen would go along with the Germans and their anti-Semitism?[5] Many did, even as Corrie and her family noticed Jewish neighbors disappearing — and to where, they weren't sure.

Corrie, Betsie, and their father began to discuss how they might help their Jewish neighbors, if given an opportunity. Willem, they knew, would be the one to ask for ideas, since he had been procuring hiding places for Jews from the start of the German occupation. The opportunity came to their doorstep, however, when German troops ransacked their neighbor's business, stole his goods, and put him out on the street. The ten Booms acted quickly, spiriting him to safety through Willem, and they soon found themselves not only in the watch business but also in the business of hiding.

4   Ibid., location 1186.
5   Ibid., location 1298.

SECRET UNDERGROUND WORK

In 1942, a stranger knocked on the door of the Beje and asked to come in. Two nights later, an elderly couple repeated the request at the alley door. All were Jews. The ten Boom's reputation in the city for befriending and loving their neighbors had become an open invitation for the persecuted to flee to their home for safety. A few days prior to the first knock, as Corrie visited a local Jewish family in their home, she considered the danger they were in and prayed under her breath, "Lord Jesus, I offer myself for Your people. In any way. In any place. Any time."[6] The Lord had responded almost immediately to her prayer of surrender.

The ten Boom home became an upstart operation working within the Dutch Underground, a haven in the middle of Haarlem. They converted a portion of Corrie's bedroom into a hidden compartment. Friends with half of the city, they used their contacts to get extra ration cards to feed the hideaways. They developed warning systems should someone suspicious enter the watch shop and used code words for communicating within the Underground. They also held practice drills so their Jewish guests could get themselves and their belongings to the secret room as quickly as possible if a raid were to come.

At the time their secret work began, Corrie was 50 years old, Betsie was 57, and Casper was 82. For more than a year and a half, they put themselves in harm's way for the sake of God's people, just as Corrie had prayed. Although Corrie knew the danger they were in and had even packed a bag of essentials for imprisonment, she couldn't fathom what was to come. Later, recalling this time, she wrote,

> Oh Father! Betsie! If I had known would I have gone ahead? Could I have done the things I did?

6   Ibid., location 1419.

But how could I know? How could I imagine this white-haired man, called Opa — Grandfather — by all the children of Haarlem, how could I imagine this man thrown by strangers into a grave without a name?

And Betsie, with her high lace collar and gift for making beauty all around her, how could I picture this dearest person on earth to me standing naked before a roomful of men?[7]

BETRAYED AND IMPRISONED

On February 28, 1944, the ten Boom home was raided. Corrie, Betsie, Casper, and Willem were taken from Haarlem to Holland's Gestapo headquarters and eventually processed into prison in the suburb of Scheveningen. When they arrived at the prison, as Corrie and Betsie were separated from Willem and their father, Corrie cried out to Casper, "Father! God be with you!" Casper looked toward her and said, "And with you, my daughters."[8] Corrie would never see her father again.

After two weeks of imprisonment, a guard appeared, barking Corrie's name. Because she had been sick since the day of her arrest, coughing up blood and unable to sit up without help, the prison guard had come to bring her to medical care. When Corrie entered the medical building, she was taken to a room by a nurse who shut the door behind her and said, "Quick! Is there any way I can help?" Without hesitation, Corrie asked for a Bible. After a doctor examined her, while Corrie crossed the room to leave, the nurse hastily came to her side and pressed a paper-wrapped package into her hand. Back in her cell, she unwrapped the newspaper to find the Bible she had requested.

7   Ibid., location 269.
8   Ibid., location 2589.

That contraband Bible became Corrie's most treasured possession and would miraculously remain with her throughout her sufferings. Two evenings later, for reasons unknown, she was moved into solitary confinement. Alone, her thoughts became her primary enemies, filling her with fear and with longing for family, food, and comforts of home. But that Bible! Corrie gulped entire Gospels in one reading, as a starving man gulped food, seeing whole the magnificent drama of salvation and sustained by the Light of the World in the darkest of places.[9]

BURNING HEART

Word soon spread among the prisoners that the Allies had invaded Europe. The tide of war, it seemed, was turning against Nazi Germany. After four months at Scheveningen, Corrie was ordered to gather her things and join the rest of the prisoners on transport vehicles, which took them to a freight yard. Corrie's delight at being reunited with Betsie in the yard quickly turned to fear when they realized they were being transported to another prison — a work prison named Vught.

At Vught Corrie learned the catalyst of the raid on their home that February day: a fellow Dutchman, working undercover for the Gestapo, had betrayed them to the police. His name was Jan Vogel, and at the mention of his name, Corrie's heart filled with fury. She thought of her dear father. While in solitary confinement in Scheveningen, Corrie had received a letter from a family member, telling her that her father had died alone in a hospital corridor and been thrown into a pauper's grave. She thought of all that she and Betsie had suffered and felt the desire to kill Jan Vogel rise inside of her. But Betsie felt something entirely different.

9   Ibid., location 2768.

"Betsie, don't you feel anything about Jan Vogel? Doesn't it bother you?" Corrie asked her sister.

"Oh yes, Corrie! Terribly! I've felt for him ever since I knew — and pray for him whenever his name comes into my mind. How dreadfully he must be suffering."[10]

While Corrie stoked bitterness, Betsie chose compassion and forgiveness. God used Betsie's words to convict Corrie. That night, she breathed a prayer of forgiveness to the Lord regarding Jan Vogel, and she slept well for the first time since hatred had set fire to her heart.

'SHOW US HOW TO LIVE IN SUCH A PLACE'

As the Allies advanced in 1945, the German guards grew rattled and anxious. One night, the female prisoners trembled as they listened to continuous volleys of rifle fire. More than 700 male prisoners were executed over two terrifying hours. Soon after, the remaining prisoners, including Betsie and Corrie, were stuffed into train cars and transferred to Ravensbruck, Germany.

The women had heard of Ravensbruck — even back in Haarlem — and knew of its notorious reputation as an extermination camp. Throughout their time in the camp, the ten Boom sisters watched and listened as prisoners suffered terribly, whether from sickness, torture, or death. Betsie herself grew sick, often unable to stand during roll call. Her prayer, from her first encounter with the fleas and all that they had witnessed, was simple: "Show us how to live in such a place."

Betsie, who loved beauty and saw the best in others, was grieved to observe such vile hatred. She longed for the truth of Christ's love to be known, not just among the prisoners but the guards as well. Bedded down together with the fleas, Betsie whis-

10   Ibid., location 3281.

pered a post-war vision to Corrie: they must tell what they had seen — not merely of the brutality, but also how the love and forgiveness found in Christ surpasses the evil and hatred of the world. They must tell, Betsie implored, of God's presence with them in their deepest suffering.

Corrie and Betsie worked long, grueling hours under the guard's rigid supervision, but each night, when they returned, exhausted, to their barracks, they weren't monitored at all. Corrie couldn't understand it, but she was grateful; for in that flea-ridden bunkhouse, she and Betsie would open the Bible without fear of reprisal and read it aloud, waiting as different voices translated its life-giving words into German, Polish, and French:

> Like waifs clustered around a blazing fire, we gathered about it, holding out our hearts to its warmth and light. The blacker the night around us grew, the brighter and truer and more beautiful burned the word of God ... I would look about us as Betsie read, watching the light leap from face to face. More than conquerors ... It was not a wish. It was a fact. We knew it, we experienced it minute by minute — poor, hated, hungry. We are more than conquerors. Not "we shall be." We are![11]

One day, when Betsie was tasked with easier work in the barracks due to her sickliness, she met Corrie at the door upon her return. "You know we've never understood why we had so much freedom in the big room," Betsie said. "Well — I've found out."[12] That day, the women in the barracks had asked a supervisor to come in and settle a dispute. The guard refused to even step through the door, saying, "That place is crawling with fleas!"

In that moment, Corrie did what she couldn't have imagined doing on her first day in Ravensbruck: she thanked God for the fleas.

11   Ibid., location 3523.
12   Ibid., location 3764.

RELEASED!

Because of the physical toll on her body, Betsie could not get well. She eventually died in the hospital barracks of the concentration camp. Corrie was devastated, but she saw in Betsie's stilled face the joy of heaven, and she became as determined as ever to follow through with Betsie's vision.

A week after Betsie died, just as the war was winding down and one week before the Ravensbruck women were executed, Corrie was released upon a clerical error, as she would later discover. The divinely appointed error set her free to make Betsie's vision a reality, and that's exactly what she did.

Corrie immediately got to work, helping those who had lost their way in the crushing devastation of war. She couldn't imagine doing anything else.

> Because I had lived so close to death, looking at it in the face day after day, I often felt like a stranger among my own people — many of whom looked upon money, honor of men, and success as the important issues of life. Standing in front of a crematorium, knowing that any day could be your day, gives one a different perspective on life. The words of an old German motto kept flashing in my mind: What I spent, I had; what I saved, I lost; what I gave, I have.[13]

Corrie knew she was not the only person to be forever altered by the war. Millions of others needed hope, so she spent the rest of her life speaking about the love and light of Christ that she had known in the darkest of places. In all, she traveled to more than 60 countries, revealing what she had seen, telling of God's faithfulness during some of the worst suffering humankind could invent, and

---

13   Corrie ten Boom with Jamie Buckingham, *Tramp for the Lord* (New York: Penguin, 1974), 29.

teaching forgiveness. She also opened a home for the homeless and war refugees.

DIFFICULT OBEDIENCE

In 1947, Corrie traveled to defeated Germany from her home in Holland with the message of God's forgiveness. At the conclusion of her talk, a balding, heavyset man approached her from the back of the room, hat in hand. When Corrie looked into his face, she instantly recoiled. He had been one of the cruelest guards in Ravensbruck. She had once stood naked before him in the shower line and watched a leather crop swing back and forth on his belt loop. Not recognizing her, he extended a hand to Corrie, thanking her for her message of forgiveness.

> "You mentioned Ravensbruck. I was a guard there. But since that time I have become a Christian. I know that God has forgiven me for the cruel things I did there, but I would like to hear it from your lips as well. Fraulein," — again the hand came out — "will you forgive me?"[14]

Forgive him! Corrie thought of Betsie's suffering. She thought of her dear father. But she also thought of how Christ had forgiven her. Could Corrie do what she had just encouraged others to do? It seemed the most difficult thing. However, she knew forgiveness was an act of the will in obedience to God, so she prayed for his help to lift her hand into the guard's and forgive as Christ had forgiven her.

14   Ibid., 54.

When she obeyed, a warmth flooded her, and tears sprang into her eyes. She had never known God's love so intensely as she did then.[15]

Until her death, Corrie traveled the world, sleeping in a new bed each night, telling everyone she met of the good news of the gospel. Over and over, she told of how Christ's love extends even to the darkest places of human suffering.

Corrie ten Boom died on her 91st birthday in Orange County, California. She was buried in Los Angeles, and her gravestone is inscribed, "Corrie ten Boom, 1892–1983, Jesus Is Victor."[16]

LESSONS FROM THE FAITHFUL

What we can learn about steadfast endurance from Corrie ten Boom

SERVE GOD IN YOUR SINGLENESS. Corrie's singleness enabled her to wholeheartedly serve God. Looking back, it's easy to see great purpose in God designing her life as he did — she was the tireless hub of the Dutch Underground, and she was able to travel after the war with great freedom.

Whether we are single or married, we all need the reminder that singleness displays the gospel, in that it shows the sufficiency of Christ. Single brothers and sisters are a gift to the church and to the kingdom of God.

Read 1 Corinthians 7:32–35. What does Paul say is one difference between singleness and marriage? If you are single, what currently hinders you from wholeheartedly serving God? If you are married, how can you encourage your single brothers and sisters to discover and use their gifts within the church?

---

15 Ibid., 55.
16 Janet and Geoff Benge, *Corrie ten Boom: Keeper of the Angels' Den* (Seattle: YWAM Publishing, 1999), 199.

"GULP" THE BIBLE AS YOUR SUSTENANCE. Corrie was starved of freedom, food, and family, but what ultimately kept her alive was her contraband Bible. Corrie describes "gulping" the entire Gospels in one sitting and "living" in the truths of the Word as if they were written just for her.

If Scripture sustained these women in the darkest of places, surely it is our sustenance as we wait for our own darkness to end. In our world full of ideas, may we cherish and "gulp" the life-giving Word just as Corrie and Betsie did.

Read Psalm 1. What is the outcome for those who love the law of God? What does this person do that leads to life? How would you describe your current appetite for God's Word?

SHARE THE LESSONS YOU'VE LEARNED IN THE DARK PLACES. God prepared Corrie for Ravensbruck, but he also used Ravensbruck to prepare Corrie for her life's work. Pain led to her purpose, to share the lessons she'd learned about God in the midst of pain.

We're often ashamed of our darkest places and the pain we've inflicted or that's been inflicted upon us. However, if God has done a work of redemption in our hearts, it is our privilege to share about him as he gives us opportunity.

Read 2 Corinthians 1:3–7. What does this tell you about God? How has God comforted you? How might you share this testimony of God's comfort with others?

FORGIVE YOUR ENEMIES. Corrie made an interesting observation after the war: "Since the end of the war I had had a home in Holland for victims of Nazi brutality. Those who were able to forgive their former enemies were able also to return to the outside world and rebuild their lives, no matter what the physical scars. Those who nursed their bitterness remained invalids. It was simple and as horrible as that."[17]

Suffering at the hands of other people can lead to bitterness. But the way of Christ, as Corrie demonstrated, is forgiveness. And the way of Christ is life.

Read Matthew 18:21–35. What does Jesus say is the motivation for forgiveness? Toward whom are you harboring bitterness? What would it look like for you to depend on Jesus for help to forgive?

17   ten Boom and Buckingham, *Tramp for the Lord*, 55.

Phillis Wheatley: Steadfast in Revolution

K. A. ELLIS

This is a song for the genius child.
Sing it softly, for the song is wild.
Sing it softly as ever you can —
Lest the song get out of hand.

— *Genius Child,* Langston Hughes (1902–1967)[1]

In 1721, slave trader Playten Onely struck up a business deal that would change the course of life for hundreds of African children. His

---

[1]   Langston Hughes, Arnold Rampersad, and David E. Roessel, *The Collected Poems of Langston Hughes,* 1st Vintage classics ed. Vintage Classics (New York: Vintage Books, 1995), 198.

signature fat and round, Onely's contract requested that the Royal African Company deploy the slave ship *Kent* to capture "500 small slaves, male and female, from 6 to 10 years old,"[2] to be delivered annually to foreign shores.

It was a deal with the Devil. This legislation opened a floodgate for the capture and sale of African children in the New World. Scores of children would be ripped from their parents' arms and plunged into the deplorable conditions of the transatlantic slave system. Prior to Onely's request, the kidnappers' sole focus had been African adult males. But now, these little ones, newly introduced into the system, represented the most powerless and innocent victims of the transatlantic slave trade.

Imagine 500 captured children, stuffed like afterthoughts into the smallest and most suffocating areas of the ship's hold for weeks on end — 500 constantly churning stomachs that had never before known a rocking sea, surrounded by the sloshing stench of the vomit and feces of other naked bodies filling the ship, chained together in their own filth and misery. Perhaps worse than being chained to the misery of the living, was finding oneself chained to the dead, staring eyes of a body whose soul had departed before land was reached. Such scenes would likely be imprinted forever on these young, impressionable minds.

It was in this crucible that the strength, grace, and poetic genius of Phillis Wheatley was forged.

. . .

Phillis was around 7 years old when she was kidnapped and forced into the Middle Passage sea journey. As an adult, Phillis wrote about its horrors to the Earl of Dartmouth, His Majesty's Secretary of State for North America. In her letter, she compared the

---

2   Elizabeth Donnan, *Documents Illustrative of the History of the Slave Trade to America* (Buffalo: Hein, 2002), 257–258.

tyranny of slavery over her human will to England's tyranny over
the colonies:

> I, young in life, by seeming cruel fate
> Was snatched from Afric's fancy'd happy seat:
> What pangs excruciating must molest,
> What sorrows labour in my parent's breast!
> > Steel'd was the soul and by no misery mov'd
> That from a father seiz'd his babe beloved.
> Such, such my case. And can I then but pray
> Others may never feel tyrannic sway?[3]

How does a 7-year-old child rise from the trauma of kidnapping,
forced orphanage, and involuntary servitude to skillfully penning
these reflective, convicting, and persuasive words?

GENIUS CHILD

After being kidnapped from Senegambia, West Africa, Phillis was
purchased at auction by the Wheatley household. Her owners, John
and Susanna Wheatley, and their children, Nathaniel and Mary, displayed their wealth through Phillis's presence. She was their luxury
appendage, their "one slave owned for life." In the New World, she
was a status symbol indulged in by only 119 Bostonian slave owners.[4]

In a twist of irony, she was given the name of the slaving vessel
from which she came — *The Phillis*. Having been stolen from the

---

3 Phillis Wheatley, Gloster Herbert Renfro, and Leila Amos Pendleton, *Life and
   Works of Phillis Wheatley: Containing Her Complete Poetical Works, Numerous
   Letters, and a Complete Biography of This Famous Poet of a Century and a Half
   Ago*. Reprint (Salem: Ayer, 1988), 79–80.
4 Vincent Carretta, *Phillis Wheatley: Biography of a Genius in Bondage* (Athens:
   University of Georgia Press, 2011), 18.

region of Africa where the slavers felt "domestic help" was best "cultivated," the intent was to train her as a domestic servant. The Wheatley's daughter, Mary, was tasked with teaching Phillis the English language so she could navigate her servant role, yet the student soon surpassed the teacher in their rudimentary lessons. As Phillis began to hunger after the Christian faith, her religious and theological education was taken over by the Reverend George Sewall at the Old South Congregational Church.

The fog of culture wars hovered over denominational debates as to whether conversion and baptism of slaves should lead to freedom. This ethical tug of war would continue for decades between a nominally Christian culture that permitted chattel slavery and the Holy Spirit-led conviction that drove men like the infamously redeemed slave-trader John Newton to make anti-slavery principles the cornerstone of his repentance.

It is understandable that possible manumission made Christianity attractive to many slaves. Yet Phillis's conversion is profound and genuine, and wonder and gratitude mark her religious works. In "Hymn to Humanity," she writes,

> Lo! for this dark terrestrial ball
> Forsakes his azure-paved hall
>   A prince of heav'nly birth!
> Divine Humanity behold.
> What wonders rise, what charms unfold
>   At his descent to earth![5]

Surely it was God's providence that gave Phillis an education of such depth in a world that doubted her humanity and intellectual ability. She continued her education while she traveled as the

---

5   Phillis Wheatley, *The Collected Works of Phillis Wheatley*. Edited by John Shields. The Schomberg Library of Nineteenth-Century Black Women Writers (New York: Oxford University Press, 1988), 95.

Wheatley family's accessory. It seems that, through her owners, she had access to the personal libraries of other socially elite Bostonians, friends of the Wheatleys. This unique access would form the classical, literary, religious, and historical basis for her life and work. While the others socialized in adjacent parlors, our solitary, delicate figure was lost in a hushed elegance amid books that opened doors to other worlds.

At age 9, Phillis was reading English with fluency and ease from the most difficult portions of the Bible. No doubt, what seemed an intellectual impossibility to those around her provided dignity, identity, and comfort as she pressed into her God-given purpose. In addition to reading sacred texts in English, at 10 years old she mastered Greek and Latin, reading classic epics like Ovid and translating Virgil into English. By age 14, she was fully catechized and published for the first time. She converted to Christianity at age 16 and became a member of the Old South Congregational Church in Boston under the ministry of the Reverend George Sewall, in the tradition and teaching of the evangelical and Reformed churches.

As brilliance shone through trauma and fear, Phillis, along with other Africans who surrounded her in her literary accomplishments, confounded the narrow categories into which they had been confined.

In 1773, Susanna Wheatley helped finance the publishing of Phillis's first literary work. *Poems on Various Subjects, Religious and Moral* was issued as a small octavo in England and quickly gained popularity. The volume included a preface in which no less than 17 Boston men vouched that Phillis, the African slave girl, had indeed written the poems. Their approval was gained through a rigorous and, no doubt, intimidating interview, where she was required to prove her authorship and translate from Latin and Greek to English and create poetry on the spot. Confounding the culture once again, *Poems on Various Subjects* became a landmark achievement in American history, making Wheatley the first African American, and the first colonial slave, to publish a book of poems.

As the Genius Child grew into womanhood, so also grew her artistic reputation. Phillis produced literary works in two styles: a provincial style that dealt with the local and global issues of the day, and a classical style that echoed works like Ovid's *Metamorphoses*, Vergil's *Bucolics*, Homer's *Illiad*, and the comedies of Terence. While she was enslaved, she received half the proceeds from her published works, and the Wheatleys received the other half.

EARLY FAME, EARLY FRIENDS

Our Genius Child is best understood in light of three distinct and intimate communities that shaped her life, theology, and practice: her enslaved literate friends, the community of artists and nobility that developed as her reputation grew, and the family who owned her.

In the early days, she had two confidants whom she admired: her dearest friend, Obour Tanner, who was also a literate slave, and Scipio Moorehead, a portrait engraver and the earliest significant African fine artist on colonial shores. Tanner gave her friendship and shared experience, and the two exchanged letters as teenagers do. Moorehead lovingly rendered the iconic portrait that graces Phillis's first collection of poems, the one that defines her to this day. One imagines these friends confiding in each other their longing for freedom, as well as how their gifts could result in self-emancipation — especially for Phillis.

Moorehead, a poet and painter and genius-child in his own right, was owned by the Reverend John Moorhead from Boston. Moorehead's iconic ink drawing of Phillis, who is sitting at a writing table with a contemplative upward gaze, is typical of portraits from the era. Her portrait includes a quill pen poised over a sheet of paper and an open book and inkwell on the desk.

Vince Caretta, the notable Phillis Wheatley biographer, explains that Moorehead's engraved portrait of his friend was actually a status piece, as 18th-century books rarely included frontispiece portraits of the author, and especially not during the author's lifetime. They were costly to both produce and purchase. Caretta further notes that it was highly unusual for any sitter of African descent to appear without her mistress or master; yet in Phillis's first book, her publisher Archibald Bell shows deep respect by imploring her patron, Countess Huntingdon, to include the extravagant portrait.

With these three closely knit friends in mind, an exquisite sepia-toned scene emerges in the imagination: three enslaved Africans sacrifice their precious late night resting hours for the sake of art and literature. They are masters of their craft, hidden and shackled by circumstance — Phillis's sad eyes raised skyward, as she rests her hand upon her beautiful, sable cheek and leans atop a simple writing table, with her dear friend Obour Tanner looking on. The chatting between them is gentle and unhurried, as Moorehead patiently sketches the image, candlelight casting flickering shadows on the walls of his simple and rustic slave-quarters.

GENIUS WORK

It is clear that Phillis loved language and Scripture. Her reflections on God are undergirded by themes of redemption, biblical authority, God's image and providence, original sin, depravity, righteous suffering, the coming kingdom, and mankind's need of the Savior. With access to her English Bibles and the original languages, she understood that chattel slavery and African inferiority was not only inconsistent with the teachings of Christ through the Gospels, but also with Old Testament Israel.

In several of her works, Phillis uses Scripture to appeal to her readers' emotions and intellect, and to demonstrate that Africans and Europeans shared a common humanity. Consider these eight lines from "On Being Brought from Africa to America," in which she seemingly revisits her Middle Passage experience:

> 'Twas mercy brought me from my Pagan land
> Taught my benighted soul to understand
> That there's a God, that there's a Saviour too.
> Once I redemption neither sought nor knew.
> Some view our sable race with scornful eye;
> "Their colour is a diabolic dye."
> Remember, *Christians*, *Negroes*, black as *Cain*,
> May be refin'd, and join th'angelic train.[6]

It was common to speak derisively of Africa as "the Dark Continent." But is Phillis here writing about the dark land of the African slave, or is she communicating in code about the dark land of the human soul? A careful reading suggests a hidden message for those both spiritually and physically enslaved. Literary analyst William J. Schieck asks us to look to these two lines for clues: "Remember, *Christians*, *Negros*, black as *Cain* / May be refin'd, and join th'angelic train."

If we read casually, we might think that Wheatley is supporting the common pro-slavery teaching that the Black race is descended from Cain and is therefore marked as cursed with dark skin. However, a closer look reveals she does not name her "Pagan land," and it is capitalized. What could she be trying to tell us? Phillis certainly would have read about many Africans in Scripture, from Moses's wife to the Ethiopian eunuch. This locates God in her native Africa, dignifying Africans, long before the slavers arrived. William Schieck sheds new light on this literary device, pointing out the "indicative use of italicization for Christians, Negros and Cain," and the subtle placement of the punctuation after the word "Negros." Though grammatically correct, the italicization and comma lend an air of

6   Wheatley, Renfro, and Pendleton, *Life and Works of Phillis Wheatley*, 48.

ambiguity that names both Christians and Negroes as descendants of Cain — all of humanity — in need of redemption and divine grace.[7]

Wheatley often found ways to defeat the common belief of the day that the Black race was subhuman. She subtly reminds that original sin and total depravity infect all of humanity, rendering all equal in the sight of God, a sentiment she echoes in her "Hymn to Humanity." O'Neale calls her destruction of the Cain myth a dual "detoxification," first of the understanding of ancient biblical curse, and then of the entire race-based slavery system.[8]

When read from this perspective, Wheatley puts the Cain narrative squarely back into its proper theological context, one that is consistent from Genesis to Revelation. In doing so, she stands for accurate biblical interpretation, for the humanity of those bound in circumstance by the color of their skin, and for those eternally bound above it by the blood of Christ.[9]

COMMUNITY OF CHARACTER

Famous but still not free, Phillis was introduced to luminaries in the colonies and in England. She developed admirers and detractors from all classes and ethnicities, eventually finding herself surrounded by a group of likeminded artists, Christians, socialites,

7   William J. Scheick, "Phillis Wheatley's Appropriation of Isaiah." *Early American Literature 27, No. 2* (1992), 136.

8   Sondra O'Neale, "A Slave's Subtle War: Phillis Wheatley's Use of Biblical Myth and Symbol." *Early American Literature 21, No. 2* (1986), 150–151.

9   O'Neale, "A Slave's Subtle War," 151–152. The Cain myth presumed that Africans were descendants of the son of Cain, and therefore were ontologically relegated to his stereotypical characteristics: animalistic and lustful behavior, the stain-mark of dark skin, a cursed relationship with the earth, displacement as a landless people, and eternal servitude to the elect (and presumably White) older brother. The "Curse of Cain" was often conflated with the "Curse of Ham."

and former slaves. Among them was composer, actor, and writer Ignatius Sancho. Sancho had no recollection of the Middle Passage journey, having been born aboard a slave ship in 1729. Yet, he likely understood Phillis's constant orphan longing: his father killed himself rather than become enslaved, and though his mother survived childbirth during the horrific Middle Passage, she died shortly after they reached the slave traders' shores.

As an adult in England, Sancho rose against circumstance and self-emancipated, becoming an independent householder, and he opened a shop that became a hub of cultural activity. A distinguished and portly gentleman with plump cheeks and a kind face, he was one of the first critics of African descent to praise Phillis. He was also the first person of any ethnicity to sternly and publicly question the motives and Christian ethics of Wheatley's owners, as well as the motives of others who managed her life and artistic career.

In 1773, he wrote:

> Phyllis's poems do credit to nature — and put art — merely as art — to the blush. It reflects nothing either to the glory or generosity of her master — if she is still his slave — except the glories in the low vanity of having his wanton power in a mind animated by Heaven — a genius superior to himself — the list of splendid — titled — learned names, in confirmation of her being the real authoress. Alas! Shews how very poor the acquisition of wealth and knowledge are — without generosity — feeling — and humanity. These good great folks — all know — and perhaps admired — nay, praised Genius in bondage — and then, like the Priests and the Levites in sacred writ, passed by — not one Good Samaritan among them.[10]

---

10 Ignatius Sancho and Vincent Carretta, *Letters of the Late Ignatius Sancho, an African* (Peterborough: Broadview Press, 2015), 112.

Sancho was soon joined by notable Christian former slaves, Ottobah Cugoano and Olaudah Equiano. Together, they wrote and published Christian anti-slavery literature, all while campaigning heavily for Phillis's release. They were joined by English aristocrat Granville Sharpe, an ethical Christian attorney who was also versed in theology. Sharpe's ideas still read today more like Christian tracts than legal briefs, attempts to disciple an entire legal system into God's concept of humanity. A pivotal figure in emancipation legislation, Sharpe is also remembered for his work among the Clapham Sect of wealthy Anglican abolitionists.

These men, along with Phillis, Samson Occom, and Phillip Quaque, began some of the first recorded Christian mission work from the shores of colonial America, even though some of them never met face to face. In 1774, they published Christian tracts that funded mission work in Ghana and in the settlements of freed Africans in Sierra Leone. Their mission work began eight years earlier than George Lisle's in the Caribbean, and 79 years before Hudson Taylor departed from England to China.

Sadly — due to the worsening conflict for national independence that would become the Revolutionary War — this early mission activity was cut short as free people of color fled or defected to the British, and the wealthy fled with their slaves to the Northern countryside. Mission work would have to be continued by another faithful team, in another age.

'ANNUS MIRABILIS' FOR THE WHEATLEYS

For the enslaved in 18th-century America, there were a number of avenues to emancipation. Some saved to purchase their freedom, others took advantage of the Mansfield option[11] (argued by Granville Sharpe) that offered a tenuous freedom, and still others chose to escape. Each choice was fraught with risk and loss. Phillis chose purchase and negotiation, the method of emancipation that appeared to grant her the most freedom. July 26, 1773, marked what she called her *annus mirabilis*: her wondrous year.

Yet the greater miracle was the transformation of the Wheatley family from slave-owning to anti-slavery sentiment, within just one generation. Phillis's former owners allowed her to live with them after her manumission. Now, she supported herself, managed her own affairs, and came and went as a free woman. Upon the senior Wheatleys' deaths, she joined the Wheatleys' daughter and son-in-law, the Reverend John and Mary Wheatley Lathrop, as a genuine, Spirit-wrought family in common humanity, freedom, and genuine Christian values. Together, they moved as refugees during the 1775–1776 British occupation of Boston. The Reverend Lathrop shows their heart change:

> I long for the time when War and Slavery shall come to an end: When, not only every Sect of Christianity, but when Jews and Gentiles, when all nations of Men on the face however differing in color, and in other circumstances, embrace as Brethren Chil-

---

11   The Mansfield option, also known as the Somerset Ruling, sprang from the 1772 legal battle known as *Somerset v Stewart*. As African slaves had opportunity, they escaped to freedom between the colonies and England, only to be recaptured and sold back into bondage through any number of avenues within the system in the Americas. In 1772, a slave named James Somerset found himself in this situation and sued his slave master. Lord William Murray, the first Earl of Mansfield, ruled from the King's Bench that no one had the right to take a slave by force [from England] to be sold abroad. The ruling by Lord Mansfield is considered by scholars to be a significant blow to legislated slavery in England.

dren of one common Father, and members of one great Family. I long for the time when all flesh shall know the Lord.[12]

Phillis married soon after, and quietly entered what historians call her "silent years." She endured the external injustices and social and economic constraints that lay in wait for an African woman in colonial America. Her husband virtually disappeared from history's record, and the Genius Child — free to roam her post-colonial world, but not free enough to make her own way — died destitute.

Though Phillis Wheatley's body lies in an unmarked and undiscovered grave, she lives in the presence of the Savior to whom she committed her life as a young girl. History may have lost Phillis Wheatley for a time. But her God did not.

LESSONS FROM THE FAITHFUL

What we can learn about steadfast endurance from Phillis Wheatley

CONSIDER HOW GOD USES THE WEAK TO CONFOUND THE WISE. In God's economy, the believing outcast is often the most powerful person in society. Even today, as Christians are dehumanized around the world, no man can ever truly steal their inherent dignity as a creature first made in God's image, and then remade into the image of Christ. Phillis Wheatley shows us that a person redeemed by the blood of Christ may remain socially powerless, but still possess a spiritual power that confounds social norms, preaching the many dimensions of the transformative gospel to those in power.

Read 1 Corinthians 1:26–31. What is God's purpose in choosing to use the weak, foolish, lowly, and despised of this world? What do these

---

12   Rush family papers, on deposit at Historical Society of Pennsylvania, May, 5 1788, Vol. 24:144, 1748–1876, Library Company of Philadelphia.

same people have in Jesus Christ? Reflect on how God uses these painful places to release the supernatural grace of Christ and indict the self-proclaimed "wise and powerful."

RECOGNIZE THAT SLAVERY TAKES MANY FORMS. In America's past, we often see Christian slaves who are spiritually free yet physically enslaved, and pro-slavery Christians who are physically free yet in spiritual bondage. Many today are still trafficked against their will, forced into darkness by others who dwell in darkness. In remembering Phillis, we must ask: in her situation, who was the slave, and who was the free? Slavery can mean physical bondage against our will by other human beings, or it can be spiritual bondage to our indwelling and willful sin.

It takes the Holy Spirit's illumination of the Word of God to both realities in and among us. This underscores the importance of discipling young believers into a full understanding of the Bible from Genesis to Revelation, how it all hangs together, and how it is intended to permeate and alter every area of our lives — not merely the spiritual, and not merely the physical.

Read Matthew 3:8–12. What warning does John the Baptist give? What does he say is evidence of belonging to God? In what ways do you see the culture approving a form of Christianity that lacks biblical repentance? List some ways in which you're learning to approve what God approves and hate what he hates.

LONG FOR GOD'S GREAT MULTITUDE FROM EVERY NATION. The Wheatleys, once redeemed, saw the entire trajectory of the Bible as proclaiming freedom, unity, and dignity that was both spiritual and physical. It caused them to long for the reality of John's Revelation: saints from every nation, tongue, and tribe gathered around the throne, not just in glory, but in the here and now. The

Wheatleys began by reorienting how they thought about their family's closest relationships.

Read Revelation 7:9. Ask the Holy Spirit to convict you about any personal obstacles, prejudices, and preferences that stand in the way of longing for God's vision for a redeemed people. Pray to develop and display a genuine picture of Revelation 7:9 in your own family, church, and communities.

Susannah Spurgeon: Steadfast in Suffering

KRISTEN WETHERELL

After a busy morning of correspondence and bookkeeping, Susie took an afternoon respite in her boudoir. It was September 1880, and the turning leaves had formed a brilliant autumnal canopy over the Spurgeon's Westwood gardens. Susie often went outdoors for respite, but at present her gaze was fixed on the lemon tree across the room, which rested undisturbed and happy in its corner. Awash in a yellow beam of sunlight, a rarity in rainy London, the once-fragile tree now flourished. She recalled what she had written about the plant four years earlier:

> [My little lemon tree] has thriven in its way as gracefully and grandly as the Book Fund, and is now an ambitious, healthy young tree, preparing itself, I hope, for future fruit-bearing ...

and the dear old motto, "Spend, and God will send," will be found true and unfailing to the end.[1]

And indeed, it had been. Susie considered the faithfulness of God, whom she had come to know more intimately through suffering and service, who had never ceased to provide for her every need. Little did she know that in the next decade, her physical pain would intensify, her Book Fund would make more demands than ever before, and her husband's death would make her a widow.

Susie would indeed come to rely, even more intensely, on the faithfulness of her Savior, who would always prove to be sufficient for her, and who would never let her go.

. . .

Susannah Thompson was born January 15, 1832, on Old Kent Road in London, the only child of R. B. and Susannah Knott Thompson. Born into the upper middle class of Victorian England, Susie was raised in a society that valued education, which her parents were financially able to provide for her. From a young age, Susie's days were spent studying art, music, and literature, and she frequently traveled to Paris. From her birth until her death in 1903, Susie would have beheld rapid change in England's technology and culture — roads became railways, gas-powered light gave rise to electricity, and women's rights advanced. Susie watched London transform.

The Victorian era was also one of assumed Christianity. God was faithful to young Susie by surrounding her with many believers. In Paris, he providentially placed her in the home of a gospel-proclaiming pastor, the Reverend Jean-Joel Audebez, who educated her

---

1   Mrs. C. H. Spurgeon, *Ten Years of My Life in the Service of the Book Fund: A Grateful Record of My Experience of the Lord's Ways, and Work, and Wages* (London: Passmore & Alabaster, 1887), 19–20.

in the truth of Scripture. She was also close to her cousin, whose husband's parents, the Olneys, were members of London's New Park Street Chapel, and their friendship meant she attended the church more consistently in later years.[2] If not for the Olney and Audebez families, Susie might not have heard the gospel proclaimed, for historians are unsure about the nature of her parents' faith. The godly influence of these families pictures the importance of bringing up young people in the knowledge and love of Christ.

In God's kindness, Susie benefited from the commitment and relationship of spiritual elders who cared about her eternal need; but salvation belongs to the Lord, and one winter's night in 1852, God drew Susie to himself.[3] "The true light" dawned in her soul, as she describes her conversion, when she heard the gospel faithfully preached from Romans 10:8. She finally saw her need for Christ, and "constrained by His love, that night witnessed my solemn resolution of entire surrender to Himself."[4] Set apart by grace for the Lord and his work, Susie had no idea of the particular callings he would place upon her during her remaining 50 years. One of these callings would soon be marriage to the "prince of preachers," whom she would affectionately call the "Prince of her life,"[5] Charles Haddon Spurgeon.

2   Ray Rhodes Jr., *Susie: The Life and Legacy of Susannah Spurgeon* (Chicago: Moody Publishers, 2018), 39.

3   The precise date of Susie's conversion is unknown.

4   C. H. Spurgeon, *C. H. Spurgeon's Autobiography: Compiled from His Diary, Letters, and Records, by His Wife, and His Private Secretary* (London: Passmore and Alabaster, 1897–99; repr., Pasadena, TX: Pilgrim Publications, 1992), 2:5–6.

5   Spurgeon, *Ten Years of My Life*, 79.

DARKNESS AND DOUBT

Susie saw Charles for the first time when he preached at New Park Street Chapel as a visiting pastor on December 18, 1853. Humorously, her first impression of the 19-year-old preacher was unfavorable; she was distracted from the sermon by his messy hair, odd clothing, and "countrified manner and speech."[6]

Yet, in the new year, when Susie entered a dark spiritual season of doubt, it was Charles who encouraged her — and eventually won her heart.

From April to June 1854, Charles and Susie would become fast friends, he pastoring her through a struggle with assurance of faith. A new believer, Susie was discouraged by her many questions and uncertainties, which she initially kept to herself. But her silence over these matters only troubled her more, giving way to "darkness, despondency, and doubt."[7] Yet God intervened, sending Charles to encourage her and point her to Jesus. Susie reflects on their early conversations:

> By degrees, though with much trembling, I told [Charles] of my state before God, and he gently led me, by his preaching, and by his conversations, through the power of the Holy Spirit, to the cross of Christ for the peace and pardon my weary soul was longing for.[8]

Prior to this season of walking with Jesus, Susie had read the Bible and prayed as mere right moral actions, but now she discerned, through Charles's pastoral influence, that these means of grace were for knowing Christ, and for her joy and spiritual maturity. Readers of Susie's books and articles will notice how completely she cast

6   Spurgeon, *C. H. Spurgeon's Autobiography*, 2:5.
7   Ibid., 2:5–6.
8   Ibid., 2:7.

herself upon him and his Word — but first she had to honestly and humbly confess her doubts. Doing this led her to the cross for the assurance she was so desperately seeking, and there in the gospel, she found the truth, comfort, and freedom her soul had been longing for.

PASTOR'S WIFE

After a few months of pastoral interaction, Charles eventually shared his intentions to marry Susie. She recounts "that memorable day in June" when "God Himself united us to each other forever. From that time our friendship grew apace, and quickly ripened into deepest love."[9] Evidently, it was God's providence that brought two such different people — a city girl and a country boy — together and who would use them in mighty ways for his purposes. They were engaged in August 1854 and married on January 8, 1856.

In her new role as the increasingly famous C. H. Spurgeon's wife, Susie found blessing intermingled with trial. Charles's preaching was marked by unusual passion and power, and the Lord gave him widespread influence from a young age. After New Park Street Chapel called him to be their pastor in January 1854, his popularity exploded, spurring the church to grow and his preaching and writing to spread abroad. His acclaim meant that he traveled frequently and worked long days, and Susie often missed him. Many pastor's wives will relate to her struggle: she desired to give her husband to the Lord with joy and free him for ministry, but this was difficult when it meant being apart from him and, in her worst moments, not being the center of his attention. One biographer surmises that Susie "truly disliked" his absences and "was sometimes downcast" by them.[10]

9   Ibid., 2:8.
10   Rhodes Jr., *Susie*, 78.

Yet Susie knew that her husband had been called and gifted by God for the work of ministry. It might have taken her some time and reminding, but these downcast feelings were eventually overcome by her "[determination] never to be an obstacle to him in his ministry."[11] As a result, their marriage flourished. In fact, biographers have mused that the prince of preachers never would have survived his physical and vocational sufferings had it not been for his supportive wife,[12] who hid herself in Christ and entrusted her husband to him.

GREAT SUFFERER

Soon after their marriage, on September 20, 1856, Susie and Charles welcomed twin boys into their home. Their joy was full. But after their birth, Susie's health rapidly declined. Chronic pain began to wrack her body, and it would continue for decades to come. Called "the great sufferer,"[13] she was often confined to the home and even to her bed; yet, in her pain, amazingly Susie still invested in her family, raised her boys in Scripture, encouraged Charles through his own sufferings, and helped him prepare sermons and projects. (She actually compiled one of his first books, even though it doesn't bear her name.)

Most importantly, Susie anchored herself in God's Word. She knew that she could do nothing, not even suffer well, apart from walking closely with him. She writes in her devotional book,

---

11   Ibid.

12   In his biography, Ray Rhodes Jr. cites two other biographers who mention this fact: Lewis Drummond (page 78) and Russell Conwell (page 79).

13   Charles Ray, *The Life of Susannah Spurgeon* (Scotland: Banner of Truth, 2006), 185.

Anoint me for *service*, Lord, that, in all I do for you, either directly or indirectly, there may be manifested the power of the Holy Spirit, and the wholehearted earnestness which only he can supply!

Anoint me for *sacrifice*, so that contrary to my sinful nature, *self* may be overcome, and bound, and crucified, that Christ alone may reign in my mortal body!

Anoint me for *suffering*, if so it be your will, that I may praise you as I pass through the waters and the fires of affliction![14]

Sufferers find an encouraging example in Susie. Even though her afflictions were life-altering,[15] she did not let them consume her thoughts, determine her identity, or deaden her hope. Surprisingly, one of the ways she remained steadfast in suffering was to commit herself to the Lord's service.

SERVING IN SUFFERING

Rather than being lulled into apathy by her chronic pain, Susie spent what seemingly little she had for the sake of the gospel. Specifically, she was compelled to put excellent, biblical resources on the bookshelves of poor pastors so they could feed their flocks. Susie tells the story of the founding of her Book Fund:

It was in the summer of the year 1875 that my dear husband completed and published the first volume of his "Lectures to my Students." Reading one of the "proof" copies, I became

---

14   Susannah Spurgeon, *Free Grace and Dying Love* (Scotland: Banner of Truth, 2006), 49–50.

15   Many believe she was dealing with endometriosis, which is likely why she and Charles never had more children.

so enamoured of the book, that when the dear author asked, "Well, how do you like it?" I answered, with a full heart, "I wish I could place it in the hands of every minister in England." "Then why not do so: how much will you give?" said my very practical spouse. I must confess I was unprepared for such a challenge.[16]

Unprepared, maybe, but not unwilling. Susie gathered the "carefully hoarded crown-pieces"[17] she had been collecting for years and had enough to buy 100 copies of Charles's book. Her husband soon placed an ad in his magazine, *The Sword and the Trowel*, inviting Baptist pastors to apply for the books, and the response was so overwhelming that Susie distributed another 100 volumes the following month. Thus began Mrs. Spurgeon's Book Fund.

The lemon tree that Susie carefully tended seemed to reflect the fund's rapid, healthy growth. As news spread, she began receiving hundreds of letters a month from poor pastors, such as the note below, and, providentially, the donations necessary to send book parcels to them:

> Madam, — The very handsome present which you have so kindly sent me (Mr. Spurgeon's "Treasury of David," four vols.) arrived quite safely about half-an-hour ago ... Thank you very, very, very much for it; and for your letter with all the kindness of heart which it reveals. Whatever may be the needs and privations of some village pastors, you, at all events, are trying to minister to their joy and to make them more efficient in the service of the Master.[18]

---

16 Spurgeon, *Ten Years of My Life*, 5.
17 Ibid., 6.
18 Ibid., 29–30.

During the first 27 years of the fund's existence, close to 200,000 resources (written by Charles and others) were sent to needy pastors and ministry workers, "books full of the glorious gospel of Jesus Christ, the study of which shall enrich their minds, comfort their hearts, quicken their spiritual life, and thereby enable them to preach with greater power and earnestness."[19] God was faithful to provide exactly what Susie needed at just the right time, to the great evidence of her husband's motto, "Spend, and God will send." She wrote of this,

> Again and again has it been proved most blessedly true in my experience. I have "spent" ungrudgingly, feeling sure that the Lord would "send" after the same fashion, and indeed he has done so, even "exceeding abundantly above what I could ask or even think."[20]

Susie, the great sufferer, committed her pain-ridden days to God's service. She spent much of her time corresponding with pastors, including a hand-written note with every book parcel, and kept a careful record of the resources and money that were donated. The work brought her great joy, as Charles observed. His words below, originally written to his magazine readers, will encourage all those who are suffering, as they did his wife:

> Our gracious Lord ministered to His suffering child in the most effectual manner when He graciously led [Susie] to minister to the necessities of His servants. By this means He called her away from her personal griefs, gave tone and concentration to her life, led her to continual dealings with Himself, and raised her nearer the centre of that region where other than earthly joys and sorrows reign supreme. Let every believer accept this

19   Ibid., 45.
20   Ibid., 15.

as the inference of experience: *that for most human maladies the best relief and antidote will be found in self-sacrificing work for the Lord Jesus.*[21]

COVENANTAL LOVE AMID DISTANCE

The demand for books through Susie's fund only increased throughout the months and years, and while she served the Lord faithfully in pain, she also knew her limitations. Sometimes, the "constant pain of both head and hand"[22] forced her to cease from her labors. Other times, Charles encouraged her to slow down and rest, and often by example.

Charles suffered in his own way, dealing with gout and seasons of depression, and knew when he needed to pause from his labors and take leave to heal. His chosen place of respite was Mentone, France, where he would recuperate from gray, rainy London. But this meant that he and Susie were often separated, as she wasn't well enough to travel with him.

The formerly healthy and vigorous young people who once adventured together now suffered alone in different places. Not many wives would respond to marital separation and solitude like Susie did. Her correspondence with Charles reveals a woman of deep hope in Christ who continued encouraging her husband despite distance and respective sufferings. In one love letter, Charles wrote to his wife, "What an immeasurable blessing you have been to me, and you are still! Your patience in suffering, and diligence in service, are works of the Holy Spirit in you, for which I adore his name."[23] No doubt, their separation pained them, as their correspondence reveals; Susie and Charles longed to be together again. Yet Christ-

---

21   Ibid., iii., italics added
22   Ibid., 27.
23   Spurgeon, *C. H. Spurgeon's Autobiography*, 4:348.

likeness and godly strength marked Susie and, in turn, she made an indelible mark upon the man whom God had entrusted to her.

HER WIDOWHOOD YEARS

For the Spurgeons, marriage was a happy blessing. But the shadow of earthly marriage gave way to the substance on January 31, 1892, when Charles went to be with Christ, after ten days of intense sickness in France.

To her great gratitude, Susie had been able to travel with Charles for the first time in years, and the happy couple enjoyed three months together before he died. "Never shall I cease to bless God for His tender mercy in permitting me to be with my beloved," Susie wrote, "and to minister to his happiness and comfort during those three blessed months!"[24] Both felt temporary reprieve of symptoms — God's kindness — and enjoyed taking walks and laughing together, until Charles fell ill and was confined to his bed.

When he finally passed away, Susie acknowledged her sadness and the loneliness that would surely come, but still, she clung to Christ, her hope. She knew that Charles was with him, and she was "sustained by the knowledge that sooner or later she would join her husband where there are no more partings."[25]

It seems that God, in his faithfulness, had been preparing Susie for widowhood during the many seasons she spent apart from her husband. Her grief ran deep, but as in her response to her physical sufferings, it did not distract her from serving the Lord. In the decade following Charles's death, she continued ministering to pastors through her Book Fund; she applied her unique writing gift, compiling an autobiography of Charles's life and ministry, five devotional

24 Mrs. C. H. Spurgeon, *Ten Years After!: A Sequel to "Ten Years of My Life in the Service of the Book Fund"* (London: Passmore & Alabaster, 1895), 163.
25 Ray, *The Life of Susannah Spurgeon*, 239.

books, and numerous magazine articles; and she even funded the planting of a Baptist church. Susie pressed on, not simply because her husband would have wanted her to, but because her Savior was worthy and was not yet finished with her:

> Best of all, dear Lord, come yourself with me along life's road, today and every day! Let the abiding of my soul in you be so real and constant, so true and tender, that I may always be aware of your sweet presence, and never take a single step apart from your supporting and delivering hand![26]

After 11 years of widowhood, while steadfastly serving her Lord and his people, Susie contracted pneumonia in summer 1903. She remained until October 22, when, with her two sons by her bedside, she said, "Blessed Jesus! Blessed Jesus! I can see the King in his glory!"[27] and passed into eternity.

LESSONS FROM THE FAITHFUL

What we can learn about steadfast endurance from Susannah Spurgeon

ABIDE IN CHRIST, FIRST AND FOREMOST. Always active in God's work, Susie and Charles knew his hand of favor and were used by him in incredible ways — but an awareness of their need for him, often brought about by suffering, kept their eyes fixed on the true prize. They knew that all they accomplished could not compare to knowing Jesus. It is easy to think about Susannah Spurgeon as a great and saintly woman — she was amazing! — but I believe she would have shuddered at this and attested that only God is great. As a woman shaped by his Word, she would have counted any gift of

---

26   Spurgeon, *Free Grace and Dying Love*, 39–40.
27   Ray, *The Life of Susannah Spurgeon*, 247.

grace as for his glory alone, and any earthly accomplishment as loss compared to knowing Jesus.

Many of us need the reminder that doing *for* Jesus cannot replace walking *with* Jesus, that knowing and loving our Savior far surpasses what we might accomplish for him. In busy cultures (and in busy church cultures) we want, most of all, to abide in Christ, know him, and love him.

Read Philippians 3:7–11. Paul says the believer's ultimate aim is knowing Christ. If someone were to ask you your ultimate aim, what would you say? Does your life reflect a desire to know and abide in Christ? How so?

SERVE THE LORD — ESPECIALLY IN SUFFERING. Suffering can feel all-consuming and can tempt afflicted people to turn inward, isolate themselves, and succumb to the feeling of uselessness. But Susie's story is different. Charles Spurgeon wrote, "For most human maladies the best relief and antidote will be found in self-sacrificing work for the Lord Jesus." Apart from his encouragement, Susie may never have started her Book Fund and, subsequently, may never have known the great freedom and joy that comes from serving Christ and his people.

Human beings are innately self-centered, and suffering can cause an even more dangerous preoccupation with self. But serving the Lord and his church (in whatever ways we can) turns our gaze outward, extinguishes self-pity and apathy, and brings glory to Jesus.

Read 2 Corinthians 4:7–12. What does Paul say is the purpose of suffering? How have you seen Jesus use your weaknesses and sufferings to build his church and bring him glory?

ENCOURAGE YOUR PASTOR. Susie had a bold vision for her Book Fund: to provide as many poor ministry workers as possible with needed resources so the church could be nourished and Christ glorified. Piquantly, she once wrote, "Are these men to be kept in poverty so deep that they positively cannot afford the price of a new book without letting their little ones go barefoot? ... we at least, dear friends, will do all in our power to encourage their weary hearts and refresh their drooping spirits."[28]

How might we also encourage our pastors? How will we refresh their hearts? It may not necessarily be through financial aid and resources (though it may be), but we should look for creative ways to build up these men who spend themselves for their flocks.

Read Hebrews 13:7, 16–18. Name four specific commands detailed in these verses that will help you be an encouragement to your pastor. Is there one you want to pursue this week? What might that look like?

PRACTICE LAMENT AND GRIEVE WITH HOPE. Even many years after Charles's death, Susie's writings reveal a hope-filled believer who was comfortable with lament: "The swiftly passing years may mitigate the grievous pain of the wound God's hand gave me seven years ago, but they cannot heal it; only the same gracious hand can do that; and it seems to me He hath bound up the sore heart just enough to make life bearable, while His purposes are being unfolded."[29] This is raw and honest lament; she grieved, but not without hope. Susie often expressed her grief by putting pen to paper, while looking through the lens of God's Word. The beauty and truth of her writing testifies to a woman whom God had entrusted to walk through many fires, and in doing so, whose refining would encourage many people walking through their own.

How comfortable are we with expressing grief and practicing lament? Do we see opportunities to comfort others in their grief? Grief and hope are bound up together in Jesus Christ. Death is indeed a terrible reality but, with him, it's not the final word.

Read Psalm 13. How does the light and goodness of a believer's salvation in Christ both free us to grieve (vv. 1–4) and also transform our

28 Spurgeon, *Ten Years of My Life*, 16.
29 Rhodes Jr., *Susie*, 187.

grief (vv. 5–6)? Do you need to grieve with hope right now? Or is there someone you know is grieving whom you can encourage?

Wen Wei Chieh: Steadfast in Opposition

IRENE SUN

At 9 a.m. at the dock of Canton, Wen Wei Chieh waited.[1] After years of hope and prayer, she had finally been granted a permit to travel to Hong Kong.

Six long years prior, she had been imprisoned by the Communists for her public witness as a Christian. Under the pretext of false accusations, Wei Chieh had endured tortures and countless attempts to force her to renounce her faith. Even after her release 17 months later, she remained under suspicion and scrutiny.

---

1   Wen Wei Chieh's birth name was Wan To Hing. The name Wen Wei Chieh was given to her by a teacher after observing her unusually strong character. "Wei Chieh" means "a powerful hero," and this was the name she used throughout her life and the name by which she was arrested. She was also known as Jeannette Li after she immigrated to the United States in 1962.

At the water's edge, she stood tantalizingly close to freedom and a new beginning. Perhaps she might see her son again. She had not seen him since he left China many years ago. Only one thing now stood between her and the ship: the inspection of her baggage.

Wei Chieh's luggage held the one thing "more precious than gold" — her Bible. To the Communists, however, her Bible was a symbol of the imperialist West, subversive to the Communist cause, and demonstrated her betrayal of China. She had only arrived at the port through a tenuous chain of interventions by friends and the grudging permission of officials. Her travel permit could be quickly and easily revoked.

As people were lining up to board the ship, another traveler urged her to toss her Bible into the river. Better to discard the Bible than to be questioned, delayed, and possibly be thrown into jail again. Her heart had trembled through her many trials, but just as many times, God had given her grace to stand fast.

She thus answered, "If the Lord allows me to go, the Bible will cause no difficulty or trouble. If He doesn't want me to go, throwing it into the river will make no difference."[2] A decade before, in a similar situation, other Christians had pressed her to get rid of her Bible lest it cause complications. She had persisted then as well, "I am not afraid to carry [my Bible]. I must have it with me. If it brings trouble, the Lord will take responsibility."[3]

This was Wei Chieh's faith in God: the Lord is sovereign over all things. This was her constant refrain: she belonged to God, so she was his responsibility.

. . .

2   Jeanette Li, *The Autobiography of A Chinese Christian*, trans. Rose A. Huston (Scotland: The Banner of Truth, 1971), 346.

3   Ibid., 230. She was fleeing from Manchuria as the Communist government came into power (1948).

Wei Chieh was born in 1899. In China, baby girls, especially from poor families, were commonly cast away and left to die. But to her mother's surprise, her father adored her. He was determined that his daughter would be educated as though she were a son. He enrolled her as the only girl in the school when she was only 5 — though he was not educated himself. Even in her old age, Wei Chieh cherished the love and gentle influence of her father.

Wei Chieh's father, however, died of sickness when she was barely 6 years old, and he left behind a debt. For weeks, a creditor came and pressed the poor widow to pay her dead husband's loan, suggesting that she sell one of her daughters — which she absolutely refused to do. Her father's family would not lend a hand or allow them to sell part of their property. Her widowed mother could find no other way to quickly repay the loan.

One day, the creditor came with his henchmen, and they pushed themselves into the widow's home. They brought papers and demanded that she put her fingerprint on them. She refused, not knowing what the papers contained because she was illiterate. So they pulled her hand and pushed her forward. She desperately clung to the door frame, her two daughters hanging on to her legs.

The men finally forced her fingerprint on the papers. They then seized Wei Chieh's little sister and dragged the child away from her mother. Only then did the widow realize — to her horror — that they had forced her fingerprint onto a contract that approved the sale of her younger daughter.

Her toddler was taken to pay for her husband's debt.

Wei Chieh was now the only child of a friendless widow. Mother and daughter clung to each other for life. Then one day, Wei Chieh became ill. Nothing could bring down her fever. A distant relative who was a water carrier for the Mission Hospital urged Wei Chieh's mother to bring her to the doctor. But she refused: "People tell me that those foreign doctors take little children and dig out their eyes to make medicine."[4]

Just then, Wei Chieh asked for a drink. While her mother went to boil water for tea, this relative put the sick girl on her back and yelled a quick goodbye. When the mother came out of the kitchen, her only remaining child was gone. The determined widow ran to the hospital, thinking to herself, "If they make one move to cut her eyes out, I'll beat them."[5]

But the doctor did not cut out her daughter's eyes. In this story of mercy, the Lord used the stubborn kindness of a water carrier and the capacious heart of a doctor to save a widow and her child. In this missionary hospital, they tasted the grace of God.

LEAD ME TO MY FATHER

Dr. Jean MacBurney treated Wei Chieh at the hospital and discovered that, besides malaria, the malnourished child suffered from hookworms and other parasites. She frequently had night terrors where she feverishly screamed for her dead father. Dr. MacBurney told Wei Chieh about a "heavenly Father" who loved her, and the girl begged the doctor to take her to him. "Only Jesus can lead you to Him," she said. Upon hearing this, the girl cried out her first prayer: "O Jesus, lead me to my father."[6] Dr. MacBurney preached the gospel to her, and the young girl immediately believed.

After Wei Chieh recovered, Dr. MacBurney urged the widow to send her daughter to the mission school. Remembering how her hus-

---

4   Ibid., 23. There were many anti-Imperialist myths circulating about foreign-
     ers. Some Westerners came to serve the people, while others abused the locals
     for their own gain.
5   Ibid., 24.
6   Ibid., 25.

band had wished for Wei Chieh's education, her mother consented. Dr. MacBurney also provided shelter and a job for the widow.

The Lord gave Wei Chieh and her mother a new life. Joy and peace entered their household.

We all come to Jesus with needs and desires. The blind want to see; the lame want to walk. Wei Chieh cried out to Jesus because she wanted a father. The death of her earthly father had created an inconsolable longing within her, and in his kindness, the Lord satisfied her longing. Sixty years later, Wei Chieh recalled, "All these experiences were God's grace to me. He used sickness and death to break up [my] home. But he did not cast me off and forsake me ... He carried me to His own Home to become His child ... If He had not done this I should have followed my father in his superstition and idol worship on the way to hell."[7]

NOT OF THE WORLD

Wei Chieh's mother was baptized in 1908. Witnessing her mother's baptism stirred in her a desire to be baptized as well. She was examined by the session, but the church determined she was too young. She applied again the next year, and although she passed the examination, she was advised to wait because of her age.

Several months later, she applied for a third time. When she was told she needed to be older, she was no longer willing to wait. "I believe in Jesus. I want to be baptized as a proof that I am a Christian." When the pastors and elders laughed, she asserted, "I won't wait. Jesus said, 'Suffer little children to come unto me and forbid them not.' Why do you forbid me to be baptized?"[8] Wei Chieh was baptized the very next day. She was not quite 10 years old.

7   Ibid.
8   Ibid., 29.

Other adults at church criticized her for her willfulness: "You should not have been baptized that day ... The pastor let you leak through because you are so naughty." She retorted, "God knows I am bad, but He loves me, I am sure. This is what we Christians say is God's wonderful grace." Joy filled her heart, and she went on to sing "Jesus Loves Me This I Know" in its entirety. "You are a naughty little girl," they repeated.[9] This was her first taste of being hated by the world because she was "not of the world" — but Jesus had "chosen [her] out of the world" (John 15:19).

CHRIST'S BLOOD RUNS THICKER STILL

Blood ran thick in pre-Communist China. Filial piety governed the web of relationships in society. Sons and daughters were the "bone and flesh" of their parents. Children paid homage and performed rituals to their forefathers — dead or alive — to show their loyalty and subordination, gratitude and indebtedness.

Because Wei Chieh and her mother were now Christians, they refused to worship the ancestral idols and perform rituals for the spirits. They were accused of being irreverent and immoral, working for foreigners and worshiping foreign gods.

The world hated the newly baptized Christian widow and her daughter. Because of the Boxer Rebellion, foreigners were deported, and the missionary school was closed in 1911. Wei Chieh and her mother were forced to return to her father's family. Her father's brothers, however, would not allow them to enter the house.

An aunt took the liberty to beat Wei Chieh with a stick "representing her forefathers." She heaped upon her words of guilt, bringing up the memory of her dead father and how she dishonored him by not worshiping him. Still, the girl remained faithful to Jesus and refused to bend her knees to idols.

9   Ibid., 30.

Blood ran thick, but Christ's blood ran thicker still. Wei Chieh was now a daughter of her heavenly Father, bound to him by the blood of Christ. Christ gave his life for her, and she was indebted to him forever. Her loyalty and gratitude was to him, and to him alone.

CLAP OF THUNDER

In her teenage years, Wei Chieh pursued her studies with rigor in the hope of educating other girls in China — but her education was halted when her mother commanded her to get married. Wei Chieh's marriage was not a happy one.

In those days, Chinese parents commonly arranged marriages for their children. Her mother and another widow, widow Li, had promised their children to one another. The betrothal came "like a loud clap of thunder out of a clear blue sky" and gave Wei Chieh a "terrible fright."[10] She sought counsel from the principal of her school and other missionaries. Everyone advised her that it was best for her to submit to her mother. After a season of struggle and rebellion, she "became numb and unfeeling" and accepted her mother's decision.[11]

She married Li Wing Kwan in 1915. She was 15, and he was slightly younger. In the hands of her mother-in-law, she was "despised, scolded, and mistreated even worse than a slave." She was so ashamed and "hated the very earth because it did not open to receive [her]."[12] She dared not speak one rebellious word lest she disobey and dishonor her mother, but in her heart she prayed, "Oh, Lord, You know all this. Flow, ye tears, flow."[13]

10   Ibid., 57.
11   Ibid., 60.
12   Ibid., 62.
13   Ibid., 63.

Three years into their marriage, her husband was away pursuing his education. Her mother-in-law was ill. Wei Chieh stayed home to nurse her while also teaching at the local school to pay the bills, and while pregnant with her baby son. These were heavy burdens for an 18-year-old. After two years, her mother-in-law softened to her and died in her care.

But six years into their marriage, "thorns came up where love should have grown."[14] Wei Chieh's daughter was born, but her joy turned into sorrow when the baby girl died 18 days later. Wei Chieh fell ill and teetered between life and death for three weeks. Yet, even in this trial, the Lord helped her see his mercy in the midst of her great grief: God carried her little daughter home, where she would never meet with the troubles and sorrows of this world.

Then, within half a year, Wei Chieh found out that her husband had been living with another woman. After this, the two "were separated as heaven and earth."[15] Her little son floated back and forth between them "with no anchor, no roots, pushed about by circumstances."[16] He lacked the warmth of a real home. She wrote, "Looking into the past or trying to peer into the future, one could only weep."[17]

GOD'S WHITE RAVEN IN MANCHURIA

Strangely, her broken marriage made it possible for her to continue her education, attend Bible school, and later, become a missionary.

14   Ibid., 67.
15   Ibid., 68.
16   Ibid.
17   Ibid.

The Lord lit a fire in her soul to "tell the Good News." This became her "most important thing."[18]

In 1934, the door opened for her to go to Manchuria, where she spent 14 years. Wei Chieh was a native of the South, where the weather is warm and humid. In comparison, Manchuria was a frozen tundra. Since she was saved as a child in a hospital, she felt great compassion for orphans and sick patients. The streets and the hospital were her frequent mission fields.

During this time, China was in the throes of the Second World War, and the mission fund was frozen. Needing to support her son in medical school, along with his wife and son, Wei Chieh decided to raise chickens. Still working at the local church, she built a wooden hut in her backyard and began this new pursuit. She peddled eggs for a living, and they had chicken and eggs to eat when there were none available in the market. She affectionately called these her "white ravens" because the Lord sent them just as he sent ravens to feed Elijah.

As Communism gained influence throughout the 1940s, Wei Chieh fled from one city to another. Finally, the Communist triumph forced her family to return to her hometown in Tak Hing. In 1949, the Communist government triumphantly proclaimed the "People's Republic of China" in Beijing. They began a relentless program of indoctrinating atheism and hatred for imperialism throughout the land. Christianity and Christians were to be eradicated.

That same year, when the American missionaries fled to Hong Kong, they gave Wei Chieh responsibility for the Mission Orphanage in Tak Hing.[19] The orphanage was owned, managed, and supported by churches in Hong Kong and the United States. These foreign alliances would become the grounds for her arrests.

---

18   Ibid., 97.
19   Some missionaries did not flee. Those who stayed were arrested and killed alongside the Chinese Christians.

FIRST ARREST: SINGING PSALMS AT THE POLICE STATION

Wei Chieh was arrested twice. She was first arrested on a Sabbath day in 1949 shortly after her appointment as principal of the orphanage. The church service had just begun when two policemen arrived and called her name. She asked them to wait while she put her Bible and Psalm book into her bag.

At the police headquarters, she took out her Psalm book and began singing. "What are you doing?" the astonished guard asked. "I am singing praise to God," she answered. "This is our worship day, and while the Christians are worshiping at the Church, I also wish to sing praises."[20] She was arrested because the orphanage was falsely accused of harboring enemy spies. The judge, however, believed her explanations. She was home by 10:40 that night.

In October 1951, 60 guards came to plunder and pillage the orphanage. Wei Chieh had kept a field where she planted corn, beans, sweet potatoes, and other vegetables. The orphanage also had water buffalo for farming, hens for eggs, and small pigs for meat. The Communists took their animals and killed their two watch dogs for a feast. All the supplies that Wei Chieh had stored up for the winter — blankets, cloth, soap, rice, oil, and salt, along with her personal belongings — were stolen, and then the guards locked up the buildings and storage rooms to hide their theft.

Yet the greatest harm by the new managers was directed toward the children. They would not allow the orphans to pray before meals, and if their orders were disregarded, the managers would not give rice to those who prayed. Soon, the children stopped praying and started eating when they sat down.

The managers also commanded Wei Chieh to stop praying. But she kept on. She prayed for the little children, their teachers, and

20   Ibid., 262.

the helpers. She was constantly in prayer lest she sin against the Lord or against these people over her. "Instruct and discipline me," she would pray, "and may Thy will be done in me, in my heart and my body."[21]

SECOND ARREST: NOT HUNGRY ENOUGH TO DIE

In January 1952, the authorities came to arrest Wei Chieh when she was cleaning the cow stall. "I knew what was in store for me."[22] But God's promise comforted her: "Fear none of those things which thou shalt suffer: behold the devil shall cast some of you into prison, that ye may be tried, and ye shall have tribulation ten days; be thou faithful unto death and I will give thee a crown of life" (Rev. 2:10).

At the jail, her Bible was immediately confiscated, along with her mirror, hairpins, and the tape that Chinese women used to keep their trousers in place. With no Bible for sustenance, her "mind and spirit were famishing, strength and energy were gone."[23] She rebuked herself for not rejoicing as Paul and Silas did when imprisoned.

There were lice on every prisoner and in every corner. The cells were dark and damp, a perfect breeding place for mosquitoes. Each prisoner was given two cups of water to wash, two to drink, and two bowls of rice, one in the morning and one in the evening. They were "always hungry, but not hungry enough to die."[24] Wei Chieh was often sick with fever and dysentery. Her intestines hemorrhaged, and the glands under her right ear swelled to the size of two eggs.

21   Ibid., 292.
22   Ibid., 295.
23   Ibid., 296.
24   Ibid., 299.

Throughout her suffering, Wei Chieh refused to shed a tear. Then, when she was ill, a guard threatened to kill her. Crushed while she was already weak, she began to weep. After several days of crying and not eating, she realized that she had allowed her troubles to overwhelm her. She quickly cried out to God, "Forgive my lack of trust ... Heal my body and my spirit, and make me to praise Thee with all my heart."[25] After she prayed, she rose and ate her food. The sun shone into her cell, so she sat in its rays.

Then there was the brainwashing. Weak with illnesses, Wei Chieh would be woken up at midnight by someone shouting her name. The guards regularly summoned her for questioning at all hours of the night. Yet the authorities had not one shred of evidence that she had done anything against the law. For hundreds of hours, the guards used sleep deprivation and threats to coerce the prisoners to confess something — anything — that could be used against them. The people assigned to brainwash her were young, less than 20 years old. She had given her life to serve children; now, teenagers a little older than her orphans took pleasure in mocking and cursing her.

CARRYING THE BIBLE TO HER COFFIN

Wei Chieh was released from prison in May 1953. She had been accused of three things — spying for the Americans, stealing from the orphanage, and killing 18 babies — but the authorities could prove none of them. She refused to leave until they gave her an official document declaring she "was freed as an innocent citizen and not as a pardoned criminal."[26]

The first thing she did upon her release was to retrieve her confiscated Bible. The officer asked her, "What book is that?" "This

25   Ibid., 301–302.
26   Ibid., 331.

Book," she responded, "is the compass for my life. [Without it], I would not know where I was or where I was going and would have no power to move. It tells us the Way of Life through Jesus the Son of God ... I cannot be without it."[27]

"You are still obstinate and will not acknowledge your wrong-doings. . . . May you cherish it and carry it with you into your coffin," the man scoffed. "That satisfies my mind and heart, and I hope to carry it even to my coffin," she answered.[28] The officers in the room were disgusted by her resistance and resilience.

Though released from prison, Wei Chieh was not free. Communist spies followed her. Her son was in America, and her body was languishing from her imprisonment. She longed for the release of death. But death would not come. "Truly, God wished me to live for Him ... I am 'more than conqueror through him that loved me.'"[29]

JUST TREAT HER LIKE GARBAGE

As the days passed, Wei Chieh was troubled to witness more Christians abandoning their faith and betraying Christ to gain the world. In the face of hostility and rage, she continued to proclaim the gospel in public squares. Many church leaders criticized her willfulness. She thanked them for their concern, but repeated her refrain: "God will take the responsibility." Some pastors wanted her expelled from Christian ministry. Others demanded that she yield to Communist teachings. Just as it was after her baptism, opposition came from within the church.

Some time later, the opportunity came for her to apply for a travel permit to Hong Kong. With her history, there was little hope that a permit would be granted, but God used her physical suffer-

27   Ibid., 329.
28   Ibid.
29   Ibid., 333.

ings to deliver her. Two sympathetic neighbors spoke on her behalf, telling the permit officer how much trouble it was to care for such a sickly woman. "The next time she is sick I shall call you to come and care for her." The other chimed in, "Just treat her like garbage and throw her out; why keep her here to clutter up the place and be in our way?"[30] After more interviews, the official grudgingly granted her the permit.

Thus, Wei Chieh stood at the dock of Canton for her inspection. The Bible in her bag was the culmination of many years of trusting God. She belonged to him; she was his responsibility.

The guard took out her Bible. Surprised, he asked why she insisted on being a Christian when so many people had abandoned their faith. She replied, "I cannot, as many have done, reject the grace of God to me, I cannot refuse His love to me which is like the love of father and mother. It is my duty to love Him. Because the Lord Jesus loved me and gave his own life for me, I cannot but love Him and also tell others about God's love for them. Therefore Christians are to spread the Gospel and give it to others."[31]

Duty here is not to be contrasted with love. Duty, for Wei Chieh, was an act of allegiance and devotion, compelled by the love and sacrifice of Christ. Her relationship with the invisible God was her closest relationship, like "father and mother." Carrying that Bible was her act of worship.

IN THE LIGHT OF GREAT PROMISES

The Lord gave Wei Chieh 12 more years of ministry in Hong Kong and in the United States. She was reunited with her son in Los Angeles. She suffered a stroke while translating the account of her cruel imprisonment. Reliving those memories proved to be too much. Her

30   Ibid., 342.
31   Ibid, 346–347.

life ended quietly, far from the land and people for whom she had poured out her life. She reflected in her autobiography, "I was like a stranger passing through, but the final records of the Church will show that it was not in vain."[32]

When Wei Chieh boarded the ship, she left behind a church undergoing severe persecution. She was once asked whether the church in China would survive. Surprised by the question, she responded, "The Church of Christ is His body. He purchased the Church with his own blood. He has promised that the gates of Hell shall never overcome the Church. You ask me if the Church in China will be destroyed? How could it be, in the light of all these great promises?"[33]

LESSONS FROM THE FAITHFUL

What we can learn about steadfast endurance from Wen Wei Chieh

PURSUE A HUMBLE, CHILDLIKE FAITH IN CHRIST. Wei Chieh was a soul acquainted with grief and powerlessness. She had no power to bring her father back from the dead, no power to acquire security for herself and her mother. But in her childlikeness, she was ready to acknowledge her needs, eager to believe in Jesus, and earnestly sought her Lord. She demonstrated a childlike faith: "Truly, I say to you, unless you turn and become like children, you will never enter the kingdom of heaven" (Matt. 18:3).

Read Matthew 18:1–4. What does Jesus say is the definition of true greatness? Is there an area in your life in which you need to become like a child and pursue humility?

REJOICE IN GOD'S WONDERFUL GRACE. After her baptism, Wei Chieh said, "God knows I am bad, but He loves me, I am sure. This

32   Ibid., 227.
33   Ibid., viii.

is what we Christians say is God's wonderful grace." Faith begins when we realize we cannot save ourselves, and seeing our helplessness compels us to cast ourselves at Jesus's feet.

In the Gospels, people cry out to Jesus with their needs and desires: The blind beggar wants to see. The centurion wants his servant to be healed. The bleeding woman wants to be well. The disciples don't want to die in the storm. How did you first come to Jesus? Reflect on and share your testimony of God's wonderful grace.

TRUST THAT THE LORD WILL TAKE RESPONSIBILITY. This was Wei Chieh's refrain, echoing the prophet Isaiah's words to Israel: ". . . even to your old age I am he, and to gray hairs I will carry you. I have made, and I will bear; I will carry and will save" (Isa. 46:4). She trusted that her Father and Maker would keep her in all circumstances, even that imprisonment was her Father's will. When she fell into despair in prison (an understandable response), she repented from her faithlessness and asked the Lord to forgive her lack of trust.

Read Isaiah 46:8–10. What does this passage tell you about God? About yourself? How does the reality of God's trustworthy purposes and power both comfort you and convict you?

TREASURE THE BIBLE AS PRECIOUS AND SWEET. Years ago, some traveling evangelists visited a Christian gathering in a rural village in China. Due to the persecution and the ban on Bibles, this church had none. On that Sunday, the evangelists brought them a copy with a red cover, and the brothers and sisters wept at the sight of it. Everyone wanted a chance to touch and hold the red book. Some cradled it next to their hearts. Others placed it against their cheeks. God's Word was marvelous in their eyes.

Remember how Wei Chieh carried her Bible even when the book could endanger her. This is not the case in the West, where the Bible is so common, readily available in our pockets, on the internet, and for purchase. It can be difficult to regard something so common as a marvelous treasure — but it is, and we should.

Read Psalm 19:7–10. What words does the psalmist use to describe God's Word? How do we nurture our love for God's Word and not take it for granted?

Catherine de Bourbon: Steadfast in Oppression

REBECCA VANDOODEWAARD

At 13, Catherine de Bourbon, "princess of the blood" of France's royal line, became an orphan. While this would be a tragedy for any teenager, persecution compounded Catherine's grief: as a Protestant living in Catholic France, her mother's death meant the beginning of life-long oppression. Thankfully, her first 13 years had been ones of preparation — Catherine's mother faithfully equipped her for a life of high-ranking hardship. Persecution was almost a way of life for Protestant women in Catherine's family; for generations, they had stood up to abusive male relatives and oppressive political rule. Such a heritage proved invaluable for what this princess would face.

For the rest of her life, Catherine's faithfulness under oppression displayed her abiding trust in God's character, even when all her earthly reasons for hope vanished.

. . .

Born in Paris, February 7, 1559, Catherine entered a world in turmoil. France was growing in wealth and power, and the government saw the Reformation as a threat to national prosperity. As the Huguenot church grew, Roman Catholic authorities hounded or exiled Protestant pastors and suppressed Protestant meetings.[1] In the 1560s, these tensions erupted into civil wars that left hundreds of thousands dead.

Ironically, Catherine was named after Catherine de Medici — the queen mother who did more than any other royal to crush the French Reformation. But Catherine's alcoholic father admired her and expected his daughter to be a Roman Catholic princess too. However, he died before she was a year old, giving Catherine's faithful mother, Jeanne, full control of her upbringing. Queen of Navarre, Jeanne was stubborn, fierce, and driven, ruling her small country with skill and will.[2] Despite early widowhood, kidnapping attempts, and military attacks, Jeanne raised Catherine to love the Lord and serve the church. Yet her Protestant faith cost her dearly. Her son, Henri, was taken away and raised as a Catholic by the French royal family.

Jeanne put the Reformer Theodore Beza in charge of Catherine's education. He added Hebrew, Greek, Latin, history, and theology to the poetry, singing, dancing, and needlework typical of a princess's education.[3] His influence became critical in Catherine's life, second only to Jeanne's.

Though Jeanne was busy dealing with national government and military conflict, she was a thoughtful mother. In the palace grounds, she had a playhouse built for Catherine, and during rare free times, they enjoyed books and music there together.[4] Jeanne

---

1   "Huguenot" was the term for French Calvinists.

2   In between France and Spain, Navarre became a safe haven for Protestants.

3   George Campbell Overend, *The Persecuted Princess: a Chapter of French History* (Edinburgh: Johnstone, Hunter, & Co., 1875), 28.

4   Nancy Lyman Roelker, *Queen of Navarre: Jeanne d'Albret, 1528–1572* (Cambridge: Harvard University Press, 1968), 411.

also carefully created support networks for her daughter. Govern-
esses and ladies-in-waiting were chosen for their piety and ability,
giving Catherine mentors and role models in her own home. Before
her teens, Catherine began corresponding with Protestant nobles in
other countries.[5]

Catherine was almost 8 when Jeanne took back custody of her
son, Henri, from the French. Reunited, brother and sister enjoyed a
comfortable childhood together and became close friends. Catherine
developed a deep affection for her brother that lasted for life.

In spring 1572, Jeanne went to Paris to negotiate a marriage for
Henri. Catherine joined her at the French court, and Jeanne wrote
to a friend, "You cannot imagine how my daughter shines in this
company. Everyone assails her about her religion and she stands up
to them all."[6] She knew from experience what it took to be faithful
in such a place.

But the long-term effects of stress and poor health combined
to end Jeanne's life in Paris. On her deathbed, she left a message for
Catherine, urging her "to stand firm and constant in God's service
despite her extreme youth, to heed the good advice of the Prince
her brother, and to follow the fine example of the ladies Jeanne had
chosen to surround her." She also insisted that "her daughter the
princess be constantly instructed in [the fear of God and knowledge
of the Gospel] and ... to marry a Prince of the same religion."[7]

It was June 9, 1572.

5   Eg.: De Bourbon to Renee of Este, circa 1570, in Catherine de Bourbon,
      Lettres et Poesies de Catherine de Bourbon ... (1570 -1603) (Paris: Raymond
      Ritter, 1927), 1.
6   Jeanne d'Albret to Beauvoir, March 11, 1572, in Roelker, *Queen of Navarre*, 376.
7   Jeanne d'Albret in Roelker, *Queen of Navarre*, 389.

UNDER PRESSURE

Jeanne's wishes were ignored, and Catherine de Medici took over Catherine's guardianship. Brother and sister were kept in Paris and lived through the St. Bartholomew's Day Massacre. As Roman Catholics entered known Huguenot homes and businesses, murdering and looting, some of Catherine's own servants fell victim.[8] The king forced Henri, also representing his sister, to recant Protestantism.[9] Catherine soon sank into a deep depression.[10] Contact with Huguenot pastors, including Beza, ended, and Catherine was put under the charge of a Roman Catholic tutor who worked to brainwash his student. Despite the depression and isolation, the young teenager stood her theological ground.

Henri eventually escaped the French court, returning to rule Navarre. He repeatedly pressed for his sister's release. It came in 1576, after nearly four years. Catherine returned home as an orphan who had seen her church massacred and endured significant persecution. The people of Navarre welcomed her — she was Jeanne's daughter, and had their trust.[11] She renounced Roman Catholicism, making public profession of her Protestant faith.

By the age of 17, Catherine served as regent for Henri, who left Navarre to establish his right of succession to the French throne through war. At home, Catherine managed troops, money, and political connections. She also welcomed people fleeing persecution and granted asylum to French and Spanish, Protestant and Catholic refugees.[12] Despite the demands on her time, Catherine managed to

---

8   The massacre, which began in Paris on August 24, lasted into October, leaving tens of thousands of Protestants dead at the hands of Roman Catholics.

9   Jane Couchman, "Resisting Henri IV: Catherine de Bourbon and her Brother," in *Sibling Relations and Gender in the Early Modern World*, eds. Naomi J. Miller and Naomi Yavneh (Aldershot, U. K.: Ashgate, 2006), 65.

10   Overend, *The Persecuted Princess*, 45.

11   Couchman, "Resisting Henri IV: Catherine de Bourbon and her Brother," 67.

12   Overend, *The Persecuted Princess*, 82.

translate the Psalms into the common language. Her time in God's Word provided spiritual refreshment for herself and others. Her education had given her the ability to run a country as well as an opportunity to serve the church. Catherine also used her religious freedom to sit under Protestant preaching. Even though Beza was in France, there were faithful men teaching God's Word in Navarre.

Like her mother, Catherine suffered from migraines. The headaches were sometimes debilitating, the worst one lasting for months.[13] Jeanne's example must have influenced Catherine in this realm too: physical suffering had not slowed her mother, and somehow, Catherine managed to run Navarre despite this affliction.

Finally, Henri won the throne through a political maneuver. In 1589, he became king of France, giving up Protestantism because "Paris is worth a Mass." Catherine was devastated: "I am so distressed by it that I cannot express it adequately ... "[14] Grieved, she was also under pressure to convert; Henri placed Catherine under serious and sustained duress to renounce Protestantism. Many Protestants followed Henri's example. His conversion was a precedent for higher classes who often saw religious affiliation as a political convenience. Against this tide, Catherine "remained a devout Calvinist despite severe pressures from her brother to follow his lead in abandoning their mother's faith."[15] But her grief did not change her affection for Henri. Her letters to him echo with a broken love: "[My] dear king ... my dear king ... my dear king."

In 1590, Catherine changed how she identified herself. Before this point, she signed her letters "Catherine de Navarre," and upon his accession, Henri gave his sister more titles: Duchess de Bar and Countess of Armagnac. But that fall, she started signing her letters simply, "Catherine." It seems that in Catherine's mind, everything

13   Catherine de Bourbon to Caumont-La Force, May, 1595, in Roelker, *Queen of Navarre*, 416.

14   Catherine de Bourbon to du Plessis-Mornay, July 1593, in Couchman, "Resisting Henri IV: Catherine de Bourbon and her Brother," 71.

15   Roelker, *Queen of Navarre*, 124.

worthwhile had been stripped away. She used this simple reference to herself for the rest of her life.

'STEADFAST IN MY RELIGION'

Over the decades, Catherine's political rank meant she had to make her religious position clear.[16] Rumors of her conversion to Catholicism circulated until her death, and Catherine regularly wrote to French believers, refuting the stories: "[T]ell all good men, that I remain steadfast in my religion and that I always will."[17] She wrote to Beza of her desire "not only to continue in the holy fellowship of God's church, in which I was brought up from infancy, but also to make sure that all good men ... know and rest assured that by the grace of God I will never change."[18]

Firm in her faith, Catherine interceded for other Protestants under persecution, opening her Paris residence as a Huguenot meeting place.[19] She showed such public concern for the small Reformed church that she became the target of Roman Catholic attacks. Verbally abused from Catholic pulpits, threatened by mobs, and lied about in the press, Catherine felt the heat. In his attempt to prevent another civil war, Henri listened to Roman Catholic concerns about his sister but did not actually stop her activities.

He did, however, continue urging her conversion. Her open Protestantism was embarrassing and inconvenient. Love for a sister seemed to have died along with his love for her God. Instead of a

16   Eg., Catherine de Bourbon to Elizabeth I, 1595, in Rayne Allison, *A Monarchy of Letters: Royal Correspondence and English Diplomacy in the Reign of Elizabeth I* (New York: Palgrave MacMillan, 2012), 164.

17   Catherine de Bourbon to DuPlessis-Mornay, 1594, in Roelker, *Queen of Navarre*, 414.

18   Catherine de Bourbon to Theodore Beza, June 26, 1596, in Roelker, *Queen of Navarre*, 414.

19   Roelker, *Queen of Navarre*, 414.

valued person, Catherine became a political pawn, as Henri used his sister to attempt political partnerships with other powers.[20] He offered Catherine to Philip II of Spain in exchange for land and military support.[21] His plan failed — Philip was not interested in alliance at the price of a Huguenot bride.[22]

HOPE IN GOD'S CHARACTER

In 1592, Henri discovered that Catherine was engaged secretly to a Protestant cousin, Charles de Bourbon. He was enraged. A king could not allow private love to spoil political schemes. He arrested Charles and put Catherine under house arrest.[23] Instead of Charles, Henri pushed Catherine to choose Henri de Lorraine, a prominent and politically dependable duke. Catherine refused on religious grounds. She had no objection to de Lorraine as a person, but she could not in good conscience marry a Roman Catholic — but Henri did not care. This marriage would take Catherine off his hands, facilitate a political treaty, and necessitate her conversion.[24]

Sickness and stress turned Catherine to writing poetry. The first poem, a set of sonnets, is a heart cry to God in the middle of deep trial:

> God, who deigns to keep in your sacred vessels
> The tears of those whom you know to be faithful ...

---

20 Roland Bainton, *Women of the Reformation in France and England* (Minneapolis: Fortress Press, 2007), 75.

21 Overend, *The Persecuted Princess*, 56.

22 Catherine de Bourbon in Overend, *The Persecuted Princess*, 58.

23 Roelker, *Queen of Navarre*, 412; Couchman, "Resisting Henri IV: Catherine de Bourbon and her Brother," 68.

24 Henri IV to Caumont, June 18, 1598, in Couchman, "Resisting Henri IV: Catherine de Bourbon and her Brother," 66.

With your eye of pity, look on my labour,
Give some relief from these mortal pains,
Or if it pleases you, Lord, that I suffer them,
Strengthen my heart against all these attacks.

Let the tears, the cries, the sighs which my soul
Brings forth in her grief, increase the flame
Which your unfeigned zeal kindles within me.[25]

The stress affected Catherine physically. She suffered from viruses and migraines and wrote that her skin looked dark and her hair was lifeless.[26] Her mental health was also affected. New persecution reopened old trauma: "And all that my bad memory gives over to me / Only serves to increase the pain that presses me, / Giving me back pain before my eyes."[27]

Unconcerned, Henri used all of his power to force the union. Catherine turned to Beza, "one of the oldest friends and servants of our house."[28] But Beza was more than a friend and servant by this point: he became her spiritual mentor once again. Catherine asked him for prayer, for his evaluation of her writing, and confessed how difficult she found her situation to be.

Her knowledge of God's character was the predominant spiritual reality that gave her perspective and the ability to remain steadfast under human attacks. Her amazement at God's grace to her kept her persecution in perspective: "I hope in your goodness, not in

25 De Bourbon, "Sonnets de Madame" in de Bourbon, *Lettres et Poesies de Catherine de Bourbon*, 206.

26 De Bourbon, "Stances D'elle Mesme" in de Bourbon, *Lettres et Poesies de Catherine de Bourbon*, 208.

27 Ibid.

28 De Bourbon to Beza, January 26, 1596, in De Bourbon, *Lettres et Poesies de Catherine de Bourbon* (Paris: Edouard Champion, 1927), 125–126.

my innocence."[29] This conviction did not stop the pain and grief but gave her strength to endure both.

On previous occasions, Henri had told Catherine that she had freedom to marry, and she reminded him of this promise several times.[30] She hoped that his affection and pity for her would convince him to let her make her own choice. She was wrong. Sister stood up to brother for years until 1597, when she finally agreed to the marriage.[31]

What Catherine would not agree to was Romanism. She knew that the king had the authority to choose her husband. However, "[In] matters of religion, she acknowledged no such right, and there was no limit to her resistance ... "[32] Negotiations with the groom's family and the pope pushed the wedding back.

During the delays, in 1598, Catherine gave France a lasting gift. Negotiations surrounding the Edict of Nantes, a religious freedom treaty, were tense. Henri gave his sister the job of convincing cardinals and bishops to support the Edict.[33] This situation involved more pressure, but of a different kind. One noble commented, "She will need to exercise her command of the arts of persuasion to the utmost ... surely no woman has ever undertaken a more difficult task."[34]

The Tuileries Palace, where Catherine lived, opened to high-ranking Roman Catholic clergy. The princess wined and dined her religious opponents, conversing and convincing off-record. When charm failed, Catherine used her position as the king's sister

29 De Bourbon, "Sonnets" in de Bourbon, *Lettres et Poesies de Catherine de Bourbon*, 206–207.

30 See for example Catherine de Bourbon to Henri IV, September 22, 1595, in Couchman, "Resisting Henri IV: Catherine de Bourbon and her Brother," 69.

31 Roelker, *Queen of Navarre*, 413–414.

32 Couchman, "Resisting Henri IV: Catherine de Bourbon and her Brother," 70.

33 Noel Gerson, *The Edict of Nantes* (New York: Grosset and Dunlap, 1969), 119.

34 Duc de Montmorency to the Duchess de Montmorency, 1598, in Gerson, *The Edict of Nantes*, 119.

to remind people that it would be difficult for their sons to gain government posts if Henri could not count on their support.[35] She also reminded the Catholics that her brother had been gracious to those who had opposed his right of succession, allowing them to retain their government posts instead of charging them with treason.

Opposition fell silent, and the edict became law. The civil wars were over. For more than nine decades, French Protestants would practice their faith with legal protection because of Nantes and Catherine's influence.

Months after the edict was signed, Catherine married de Lorraine. Henri promised that if she did, she would no longer be under pressure to convert and could bring her Huguenot servants with her.[36] But shortly after the wedding, de Lorraine worked with the king to isolate his bride, dismissing her Protestant ladies-in-waiting and replacing her Huguenot pastor with priests. Catherine, recovering from a serious fever, was devastated: "a blow so cruel and hard to believe … I cannot imagine that after obeying you … in taking a husband of the other religion … you would do such a cruel thing … Have pity on a little sister … I can bear everything else, but this reduces me to despair."[37]

PERSEVERANCE AMID GRIEF

As a teenager, Catherine withstood similar pressures. Now, with severe disappointments and decades of weariness on her shoulders, Catherine needed pastoral care to endure. Beza was still there for her, a faithful correspondent and pastor. In the summer of 1599, at

---

35   Gerson, *The Edict of Nantes*, 122.
36   Couchman, "Resisting Henri IV: Catherine de Bourbon and her Brother," 71–72.
37   Catherine de Bourbon to Henri IV, March, 1599, in Roelker, *Queen of Navarre*, 414–415.

40 years old, Catherine suffered a miscarriage.[38] She wrote to Beza, assuring him that her health was good and that she was not flagging in her commitment to the Reformed faith. But she knew that she needed supernatural support: "I beg you to assist me with your holy prayers ... "[39]

She longed for a baby. Aware that the likelihood of having a child was slim at her age, Catherine did what she could to facilitate conception.[40] Her poor health did not help, neither did the stress of a complicated marriage. Infertility seems to have been a constant grief, sometimes central, sometimes pushed to the side, but always present. Perhaps the close relationship with her mother brought hope of a similar love between herself and a child, and the loss of this hope wore her down emotionally.

Ongoing intercessions with the pope added to the pressure for Catherine to convert. Henri worked for years to chip away at her resolve, but with no effect: "we have not been able to defeat my sister the Duchess de Bar, with all our efforts and means ... I have spared neither advice nor persuasion, nor the authority I have over her ... "[41] At one point, Catherine responded to Henri's arguments by saying, "Sire, they wish me to believe our mother is damned!"[42] Jeanne's example of faith continued to give Catherine strength.

38   De Bourbon to Henri IV, August 18, 1599, in Roelker, *Queen of Navarre*, 415.

39   De Bourbon to Beza, July 23, 1599, in de Bourbon, *Lettres et Poesies de Catherine de Bourbon*, 163.

40   At the turn of the 16th century, this meant "taking the waters" at "healthy" places, eating certain foods, and praying.

41   Henry IV to Monsieur de Bethune, March 21, 1602, in Couchman, "Resisting Henri IV: Catherine de Bourbon and her Brother," 73.

42   Overend, *The Persecuted Princess*, 107.

PURPOSE IN TROUBLE

More than anything, Catherine's trust in God's goodness — that God was good and would do good — sustained her. Time and again in her poetry, she places herself at the mercy of his character. He continued to save her from the flesh; surely he would keep her from succumbing to the world and the Devil.

In fall 1599, Catherine wrote to Beza that she had endured many "assaults, but God has always strengthened me. I hope he will give me the grace to complete my race for his glory and my salvation."[43] Help was not limited to the spiritual (in the same letter, Catherine asked Beza's advice about some jewels), but spiritual aid was the mainstay. In December, Catherine wrote to Beza as "your very affectionate friend," "assisted by a special grace of God" despite "all kinds of afflictions." She asked him to pray for a "diminution to my ills, or an extra-ordinary force to bear them."[44]

Perhaps just writing to Beza — focusing her thoughts and expressing them to a pastor — gave her comfort. But Beza was not a passive listener. Catherine thanked him "very much for … the admonitions which you give me by your letters … " They contained not only "solace" but also "obligation."[45] Catherine was suffering, but that did not make her perfect. In the middle of "unbearable trouble," Beza apparently thought it appropriate to give some kind admonition and spiritual challenge along with his encouragement,[46] which Catherine could take from a man whom she trusted, who bore

---

43   De Bourbon to Beza, October 15, 1599, in de Bourbon, *Lettres et Poesies de Catherine de Bourbon*, 171.

44   De Bourbon to Beza, December 2, 1599, in de Bourbon, *Lettres et Poesies de Catherine de Bourbon*, 174.

45   De Bourbon to Beza, September 24, 1600, in de Bourbon, *Lettres et Poesies de Catherine de Bourbon*, 177.

46   De Bourbon to Beza, December 15, 1600, in de Bourbon, *Lettres et Poesies de Catherine de Bourbon*, 179.

her burdens with her. In her last letter to Beza, she wrote that the knowledge of his daily prayers on her behalf was her "consolation."[47]

Letters show that despite the tensions and differences, husband and wife genuinely cared for each other. Increasingly caught between theological conviction and relational commitment, they lived apart for a time.[48] Tense relationships, isolation, poor health, and the grief of infertility combined to make life unwelcome for Catherine: "I swear before God that I wish for death a thousand times a day."[49]

But things began to resolve relationally as husband and wife moved back in together. The pope offered to recognize the marriage as legitimate as long as any children were raised as Roman Catholics. Catherine made no public response. It was early 1604, and she thought that she was expecting again. Sick with tuberculosis, she would take no medical help in case it hurt the baby. But the growth was an abdominal tumor that ended her life on February 13 of that year. She never realized what was really happening and died begging the doctors to save her child.[50] Henri did not attend her funeral.[51] Her body was buried beside her mother.

WORTHY OF TRUST

Catherine's steadfastness was not coincidence. It was not even a family trait. It was an expression of the reality that because of who God is, he is worthy of our trust even when life makes no sense.

---

47   De Bourbon to Beza, December 6, 1603, in de Bourbon, *Lettres et Poesies de Catherine de Bourbon*, 196.

48   Couchman, "Resisting Henri IV: Catherine de Bourbon and her Brother," 73.

49   Catherine de Bourbon to Henri IV, August 7, 1600, in Bainton, *Women of the Reformation*, 80.

50   Bainton, *Women of the Reformation*, 81.

51   Roelker, *Queen of Navarre*, 416. Six years later, Henri was assassinated.

Her stewardship of this inheritance, especially in oppression, was a faithful and fruitful one.

> Gentle and good Father, who knows everything,
> Do not close your eyes to my eyes full of tears;
> Look at my troubles from your high heavens
> And do not close your ears to my sad cries.
>
> O God, I rest on all your goodness;
> With a humble heart I lift up my vows.
> Do with me, O Almighty, what you wish …
>
> … worldly pleasures have no power over me,
> Property or grandeur do not shake my faith,
> My dearest care is to live in your fear.[52]

LESSONS FROM THE FAITHFUL

What we can learn about steadfast endurance from Catherine de Bourbon

SEEK TO TRAIN YOUNG BELIEVERS IN THE FAITH. When Catherine faced persecution, betrayal, and other hardships, she had a theological framework that enabled her to think and therefore act in biblical ways. This was largely the fruit of her mother's training and Beza's teaching.

Read 2 Timothy 1:1–7. What do you learn about Timothy's faith from this passage? How can we be diligent about teaching children or younger Christians in our lives?

---

52   De Bourbon, "Sonnets de Madame … qu'elle a composes Durant sa maladie," 1595, in De Bourbon, 206–207.

TRUST GOD'S PURPOSE IN YOUR POSITIONS OF INFLUENCE.
Catherine's involvement with the Edict of Nantes was crucial. She
acted for the church, not herself, as Nantes was pushed through despite "violent opposition."[53] Like Esther, Catherine used her political position to protect her people, even at risk to herself. The Lord
blessed this work, giving his people freedom, even though Catherine
never enjoyed it.

*Read Esther 4:12–16. We all naturally avoid painful things, espe-
cially when we are in a position to choose comfort and security. What do
you learn from Esther's example? In what areas of life does Jesus want
you to move toward discomfort for the sake of his people?*

ENCOURAGE, AND BE ENCOURAGED BY, OTHER BELIEVERS.
Catherine was a great encouragement to contemporary believers.
Her public position and refusal to cow under pressure made her
a model to other French Protestants suffering similar things. She
wanted the Huguenot church to know, "I am resolved to live and die
in the only religion in which I believe."[54]

*Read 2 Timothy 1:8–14. Like Paul, Catherine could tell other
believers to follow her as she followed Christ. In what ways are you living
a Spirit-dependent life, guarding the good deposit entrusted to you? In
what ways can you encourage others to stand strong in their faith in the
midst of hardship or persecution?*

TRUST GOD'S GOODNESS THROUGH SUFFERING. Perhaps the
most remarkable aspect of Catherine's life is her abiding consciousness of God's goodness to her, despite outward circumstances. Her
first poem focuses on something more personal and fundamental
than persecution: "My sin displeases me; forgive me, Lord . . . I hope
in your goodness, not in my innocence."[55] God's goodness, though

---

53 Roelker, *Queen of Navarre*, 414.
54 De Bourbon to the Duke de Bouillon, June, 1597, in Couchman, 71.
55 De Bourbon, "Sonnets," 206–207.

sometimes veiled and not expressed as expected, did not fail her. In fact, her continual desire and ability to cry out to him was evidence of his goodness. Satan's attacks were unable to distort her view of her Savior.

Read Matthew 26:36–42. If Jesus suffered in obedience to the Father, we can expect suffering, too. But we can also expect the suffering to do what it is designed to: make us like Jesus. How has God used your sufferings to make you more like himself? How does trust in God's goodness make us able to say, "Not my will, but yours be done?"

Lilias Trotter: Steadfast in Adversity

JEN OSHMAN

Draped in linens from head to toe, the woman peeked out through the opening in her headdress. Bewildered by the sight of a European visitor, she asked, "What do you want?"

"I love the Arabs and have come to have a talk with you."[1]

The year was 1893, and Lilias Trotter, along with her friend and co-laborer Blanche Haworth, had ventured for the first time from the city of Algiers into the Sahara Desert. The two women were on mission to proclaim the gospel in remote Muslim communities. They had been in Algeria since 1888, but this was their first expedition into the desert.

The journey required long days, courage, and conviction. The women started by rail, transferred to horse-drawn cart, and then entrusted themselves to an unknown guide who led them into the Sahara by camel. The temperatures threatened to sear their lungs, the sun and sand to burn their skin, and sandstorms to erase their path.

---

1   Blanche A. F. Pigott, *I. Lilias Trotter* (London: Marshall, Morgan & Scott Ltd., 1929), 40.

Dehydration was imminent, and an awareness of bandits, scorpions, wild dogs, and unknown diseases was necessary for survival.[2]

Amid all these threats, however, Lilias perceived that the greatest danger was to human souls: "Oh, the awful need of the world! It presses on one coming to a new ground like this."[3] As the spiritual darkness of Algeria enveloped her, she pressed further on and into crowded city streets, remote villages built into mountainsides, and isolated tent communities in faraway corners of the desert.

She was thrilled to be the first to announce the grace of Jesus to those who knew nothing of him.

In a 1909 prayer booklet, Lilias painted a picture of an unfamiliar flower: the sand lily. As she so often did, she added words of devotion:

> Today's find was beautiful to the inward vision as well as to the outward. It was clusters of exquisite wild lilies — white and fragile and fragrant — growing out of the hot salt sand that drifts into dunes ... Down below the surface, the storage of reserve material in the lily bulbs had silently taken place ... The hour had come now, and no adverse condition could keep back the upspringing. The same Lord over all can store the roots in His spiritual creation, even though they have but smothering sand drifts around them.[4]

Though Lilias poured herself out and saw no spiritual fruit among the Algerians for years, she had faith that the Lord of creation was nourishing a storage of reserve material in the hearts of fu-

---

2   Miriam Huffman Rockness, *A Passion for the Impossible: The Life of Lilias Trotter* (Grand Rapids: Discovery House Publishers, 2003), 136–137.

3   Pigott, *Lilias*, 43.

4   Miriam Huffman Rockness, *Images of Faith: Reflections Inspired by Lilias Trotter* (Naples: Oxvision Books, 2019), 92.

ture believers. She believed that work was being done down below the surface.

Lilias found the Algerians and the sand lily analogous,[5] but so too were Lilias and her flower.[6] Known as Lily to her friends, the Lord planted in her a secret storehouse of strength to carry her through 40 years of service to him in North Africa. Her pioneering work culminated in the formation of the Algiers Missions Band, now known as Arab World Missions.

. . .

Lilias Trotter was born into a wealthy Victorian household in London's well-to-do West End in 1853. Her father, Alexander Trotter, was a successful stock broker from a young age. Her mother, Isabella, was known to be warmhearted, an evangelist for Christ, and an advocate for the oppressed.[7]

Like others in their Regent Park community, the Trotters enjoyed dinner parties with artists, writers, and the social elite. Lilias was tutored at home in languages, art, and music, enjoyed day trips about London, and took vacations abroad. The family was active in the Church of England and known for their kindness. Like the unseen bulb of a sand lily, Lilias received ample nourishment in her earliest years.

Alexander Trotter passed away when Lilias was 12, testing her heart and faith. Aching for her earthly father, she held tightly to her heavenly Father. From then on, she was often found praying in her room or in the garden. A deep and personal faith had taken root.

Lilias cultivated her faith by attending spiritual conferences and campaigns that were popular in England at the time. In the

---

5   Ibid., 93.
6   Ibid. I am indebted to Miriam Rockness for first drawing the parallel between Lilias and the sand lily.
7   Rockness, *Passion*, 38.

greenhouse of Christian community, she made influential lifelong friendships, drew nearer to her precious Lord Jesus Christ, and fostered a drive to work out her faith in service and the proclamation of the gospel. She even received training from the famous American evangelist Dwight L. Moody, who visited London, hosted evangelistic campaigns there, and taught Christians how to use the *Wordless Book* to explain the plan of salvation.[8] Lilias had no idea that the relationships, faith, and skills grown in this sweet season would bear fruit decades later in Algeria.

DUELING ACTS OF WORSHIP

Lilias's young adult life was marked by two competing passions: the pursuit of fine artistry and ministering to the poor in London. From a young age, Lilias saw nature as an important way of seeing and knowing God. He imparted to her an exceptional ability to capture people and places in painting and drawing.

Her artistic gifts were so unusual that Lilias gained the attention of John Ruskin, a preeminent art critic and social philosopher of the Victorian age. Ruskin saw in her an unprecedented gift and thrilled to see her embrace his instruction over the span of several years. Lilias, too, delighted in nurturing this God-given skill.

Ruskin was so convinced of Lilias's talent that he told her "she would be the *greatest living painter* and do things that would be *Immortal.*"[9] His affirmations and drive to train her full-time, along with her own love of art, led to a crisis of faith: her delight in

8   Noel Piper, *Faithful Women and their Extraordinary God* (Wheaton: Crossway, 2005), 44. Piper credits Charles Spurgeon with first introducing the idea of a *Wordless Book* in a sermon in 1866. Lilias learned the idea from Moody in 1875.
9   Rockness, *Passion*, 83 (italics added).

art was matched by her delight in serving the Lord and his people in London.

Lilias viewed both her artistic and ministry endeavors as gifts from God. Yet she felt she could not fully give herself to both ambitions.

LILIAS'S CHOICE

The decision tormented her: "[It's] an almost constant state of suffocation half intoxication so that I can hardly eat or sleep except by trusting the Lord about it, if I had not Him to hide in deeper than ever before, I don't know what I should do. ... I do believe Christ will win in the end."[10]

Ultimately, Lilias chose ministry over art. She knew this would mean being misunderstood, even maligned: "I see as clear as daylight now, I cannot give myself to painting in the way [Ruskin] means and continue to 'seek first the Kingdom of God and His righteousness.'"[11]

Walking in the freedom of obedience to Christ, Lilias served in prayer groups, volunteer forces, choirs, Bible classes, the Young Women's Christian Association (YWCA), and multiple ministries in London's poorest neighborhoods for nearly a decade.[12] Forsaking her precious Victorian reputation and even her eligibility for marriage, Lilias spent nights walking the streets, extending kindness and care to the women of London's lowest classes. She welcomed them into a Christian home for a meal, a good night's sleep, training in a marketable skill, and an invitation to Jesus.

Lilias underwent minor surgery in 1884. The details surrounding her health and the need for the surgery remain a mystery. In a

10   Ibid., 84.
11   Pigott, *Lilias*, 11.
12   Piper, *Faithful*, 47.

letter to her dear friend Blanche, Lilias writes, "Dr. Bennet can't quite make out what is wrong with me."[13] The surgery led to a forced period of rest and unexpectedly weakened her heart for the rest of her life. What was meant to be a small medical procedure became a lifelong thorn in her flesh (2 Cor. 12:7), requiring her to reconcile the demands of ministry with the frailty of her body for decades to come.

CALL TO NORTH AFRICA

Fully engrossed in her service in London, Lilias gave little thought to the pioneering mission work that was happening overseas. However, she noticed that two dear friends "had a fellowship with Christ over His work in the dark places of the earth of which I knew nothing, and the cry rose unbidden with a curious persistence, 'Lord, give me the fellowship with Thee that those two have.'"[14]

The Lord answered: North Africa inexplicably became central to Lilias's thoughts and prayers. She attended a missions meeting where someone in attendance asked, "Is there anyone in this room whom God is calling for North Africa?" Prompted by the Holy Spirit, Lilias responded, "He is calling me."[15]

Less than nine months later, Lilias set out. She didn't have the support of a missions agency, as her heart condition prevented her formal acceptance. But she did have the financial means to support herself, as well as two dear friends, Blanche Haworth and Lucy Lewis, who set out with her — all eager to shine the light of Christ in Algeria.

Nothing could keep the inward growth God had been nourishing in Lilias from "upspringing" at the appointed hour.

13   Pigott, *Lilias*, 13.
14   Emily Kinnaird, *Reminiscences* (London: Murray, 1925), 57.
15   Pigott, *Lilias*, 15.

ARRIVAL IN ALGERIA

On March 10, 1888, Lilias recorded, "I shall never forget the loveliness of our first sight out of our port-hole of the Arab town rising tier above tier in a glow of cream colour against the blue-grey western sky, the water glimmering in blue and gold below, and a flock of gulls sailing and wheeling alternately between us and the land."[16] As the ship docked, the brand new missionaries sang "Crown Him Lord of All," affirming the very reason they traveled to these foreign shores.

Algeria had been dominated by Islam for a millennium and colonized by the French for 60 years. Lilias and her tiny band knew little about the country; they spoke not a word of Arabic; they didn't have a mission agency or mentors to help them; and all three were burdened by health issues.[17] As soon as they arrived at their temporary lodging, they began with all they had: prayer.

What the women lacked in preparation, they made up for in zeal. Employing a French-Arabic dictionary, Arabic classes, and tutors, they devoted themselves to learning the language, that they might communicate the gospel. They asked their Arabic teacher to translate small portions of Scripture onto decorative pieces of paper that they passed out to men in the cafes. While perhaps seemingly reckless compared to today's missional strategies, these enthusiastic methods produced the Algiers Mission Band's first conversations and relationships.

The strength and unity of Muslim culture was an unseen wall, keeping out the new missionaries. Whether in the city of Algiers or far out in the desert, the people were bound by language, fasts and feasts, calls to prayer, and strict gender roles. Arab women, for example, were not allowed in public. Lilias learned that to gain access to the women, she must establish trust and friendship with their

16   Ibid., 20.
17   Rockness, *Passion*, 109.

children, who would then invite her into the fortressed home where she might share God's love with multiple wives and children.

GOSPEL URGENCY

In pursuit of lost hearts, Lilias and her colleagues moved into the Arab quarter of Algiers. A friend who visited from England said, "I shall never forget my first impression of that narrow street where Miss Trotter dwelt; a dust storm was blowing ... dirty papers, and rubbish flying all around, it looked utterly squalid."[18] In contrast, Lilias said, "It was good ... to plunge down among the crowds."[19]

Gospel urgency compelled Lilias and her band to visit countless communities throughout the Sahara and along the Atlas Mountain Range. Lilias proclaims, "Oh, it is wonderful to be allowed to break the silence in which God has been loving them all the time."[20] The missionaries thrilled at these first tiny shoots — "fragile and fragrant, growing out of the hot salt sand that drifts into dunes."

With agility and decades-long stamina, the women created and adjusted countless outlets for sharing the gospel. They offered embroidery and Bible classes to women and girls, special teas for their Arab water carriers, and open houses for Arab women on the unique days when they could leave their homes to visit the cemetery. They brought medicine, along with gospel literature written in Arabic and decorated with Arabic designs, to remote desert and mountain communities. They hosted camps for Arab families to get away and hear the gospel, and served as matchmakers for new young adult Christians. They also hosted short-term mission teams from Europe and traveled abroad to spread word of North Africa's needs. They

18   Piggott, *Lilias*, 85.
19   Ibid., 44.
20   Ibid., 50.

organized missions conferences and helped with the translation of Scripture into colloquial Arabic.

GOSPEL OPPOSITION

Each spiritual sprout was a celebrated victory, as evil and opposition were "smothering sand drifts around them." In North Africa, sorcerers would seek to "cure" new believers — or pursue revenge — by black magic. New Christians were often threatened by poison, concocted by a sorcerer employed by the new believer's family. The drugs secretly administered in their food caused them to be highly suggestible, open to hypnotism, and unable to think clearly. Each year during Ramadan, new Christians were harassed and closely watched to ensure that they followed the Muslim fast. Those who chose Christ over Islam were persecuted.

Within a few years of living in Algeria, the women noticed that every March — the month in which they first landed — was rife with hardship. Thirty years after their arrival, Lilias writes of her dearest friend, "Blanche is still ill.... a curious feeling hangs over it ... we are close on the early days of March that have been almost invariably marked by some contest, as if the powers of darkness remembered that they were the date of our coming out for the first time."[21] Indeed, on March 9, 1918, the anniversary of their arrival, Blanche Haworth passed away. But Lilias and her remaining colleagues pressed on, believing that nothing could keep back the "upspringing" that God was growing below the surface.

Lilias faced adverse conditions that were not only external. Her weak heart required daily, weekly, and annual habits of rest. She spent those hours and days reading the Bible, praying, and listening for the direction of the Holy Spirit. The fruit of Lilias's inward rest was the outward vision of clusters of exquisite wild lilies: hundreds

21   Rockness, *Passion*, 263–264.

of booklets, leaflets, parables, and books, as well as hundreds of sketches and paintings, all produced for the love of God and people. It's no wonder that the popular hymn "Turn Your Eyes Upon Jesus" was inspired by Lilias's reflections,[22] as that's exactly what her writing and artwork prompted people to do.

GOSPEL SUSTAINABILITY

In her final years, Lilias turned special attention to the sustainability of a gospel witness in Algeria beyond her life. For example, over the years she had several encounters with the Sufi brotherhood — Muslim mystics who hungered after the presence of God. She gained their respect and was repeatedly invited into their *zaourias*, fraternal settings where Sufi men gathered in their long white robes, sat among great books of the age, drank coffee, and debated spiritual mysteries.[23] Lilias spoke to them about "The Way," the gospel. Her dream was that they would come to know Jesus and then become missionaries themselves to Arab Muslims.[24] To that end, she wrote *The Sevenfold Secret*, a book addressed to the Sufi in their own style, bridging their desire for unity with God to Jesus's seven "I am" sayings in the Gospel of John.[25] Even now, Christians and nonbelievers alike in Arab North Africa seek out this book and others penned by Lilias because of their beauty, cultural precision, and inspiring content.

In 1925, Lilias's doctor ordered her to stay in bed because of her weak heart. With no thought of returning to England, she planted herself firmly in her bedroom in the Arab quarter of Algiers. From there she directed the growing native and foreign staff of the

22   Ibid., 327.
23   Ibid., 19.
24   Ibid., 272.
25   Ibid., 301.

Algiers Mission Band. She conducted meetings, assisted in the establishment of long dreamed about desert outposts, orchestrated conferences, and weighed in on strategic decisions. She handed over leadership to the next generation and rejoiced in seeing the work expand, even as she grew frailer.

LILIAS'S LAST YEARS

Reflecting on decades of ministry, Lilias wrote in her diary in 1926, "Long ago — fifty years or more in the past, it was a joy to think that God needed me: Now it is a far deeper joy to feel and see that He does not need me — that He has it all in hand!"[26]

From a position of physical and spiritual rest, Lilias labored in prayer for her beloved Algeria. She had a map of North Africa hung above her bed so that she might pray every day for the entire region. She called on the Spirit to work down below the surface, to bring forth beautiful sand lilies in his name.

In March 1928, the Algiers Mission Band reflected on 40 years in the desert and anticipated what God might do next. Three months later, on August 27, friends gathered in Lilias's bedroom and sang her favorite hymn, "Jesus Lover of My Soul." They say she looked out the window and exclaimed, "A chariot and six horses!" When asked if she was seeing beautiful things she answered, "Yes, many, many beautiful things." She stretched out her arms, lifted them in prayer, and breathed her last.[27]

Just like her flower, Lilias Trotter is a testament to our powerful God who uses weak people so that we might boast in him alone (1 Cor. 1:27–29). The lilies, Lilias herself, and Arab Christians, who trace their lines of faith back to the Algiers Mission Band, all bear

26   Ibid., 304.
27   Ibid., 324.

witness to him who grows beauty in "the hot salt sand that drifts into dunes."

LESSONS FROM THE FAITHFUL

What we can learn about steadfast endurance from Lilias Trotter

STEWARD ALL THINGS AS GIFTS FROM GOD AND FOR GOD. Lilias understood that everything she had came from her Creator. She rightly viewed her family, faith, education, wealth, artistic abilities, friends, and even her heart condition as provisions of God for her good and his glory. About her artistic gift, she writes to a friend, "I know that I have no more to do with the gift than with the colour of my hair."[28]

We are quick to take credit for all we have, championing self-made men and women. But the truth is, God "himself gives to all mankind life and breath and everything" (Acts 17:25).

Read Colossians 1:15–20. What does Paul say that all things are created through and for? What gifts, trials, and/or thorns has he given you? How are you using them for his glory?

FIND TRUE LIFE AS YOU DIE TO YOURSELF. As an artist and lover of creation, Lilias saw that flowers bud, blossom, and bear seeds and then die themselves to bring forth new life. In *Parables of the Cross*, she reflected on and painted scenes of nature that proclaim how "death is the gate of life."[29]

We are naturally averse to risk and pain, so safety and security can be strong idols for us. Yet, counter to our fleshly desires and cultural values, Christians are called to die to both of these things, that we might receive true life in Christ.

---

28   Pigott, *Lilias*, 10.
29   Lilias Trotter, *Parables of the Cross* (London: Marshall Brothers, 1895), 6.

Read Matthew 16:24–28. What does Jesus say to those who want to follow him? In what ways are you laying your life down for the sake of others and the glory of God?

SPEND TIME IN GOD'S WORD AND PRAYER IN ORDER TO KNOW AND TRUST HIM. Reflecting on the eagle who at first depends on his mother for food and help, and then sets out on his own, Lilias writes, "[It] is an older faith that learns to swing out into nothingness and drop down full weight on God ... that is trained faith."[30] It was trained faith — one that knew well its Maker and Sustainer — that carried Lilias along.

In an age that values productivity, it's tempting to forego time with the Lord so we can get busy. But there's no shortcut to intimacy and trust. We cannot trust whom we do not know.

Read Luke 10:38–42. According to Jesus, what is "the good portion," the "one thing [that] is necessary"? Where do you see yourself in Mary and Martha's story?

GO AND MAKE DISCIPLES OF ALL NATIONS — WITH JOY. In 1923, when Lilias was 70 years old, she made her final journey into the southern desert to proclaim Christ. The Souf people were so thrilled to hear the gospel that they begged her to stay and live with them. With lament she writes in her diary, "Oh if the shadow of life's dial would go backward and make it possible!"[31] In spite of all the sacrifices she made to be a pioneer missionary to North Africa for 40 years, Lilias wished for more time.

We often view missions (whether local or global) as too costly, or too specialized, or something others are called to do, but not us. Lilias shows us that anyone can go and that there is great joy even in the difficulties.

---

30   Rockness, *Passion*, 188.
31   Ibid., 291.

Read Matthew 28:16–20. What is Jesus's command? What is his promise? Obedience to the Great Commission can come in many shapes and sizes: you might be a goer or a sender, and you might go across the street, across town, or across the ocean. What reassurance and motivation do you take from these verses? How might you apply these to a current relationship with a nonbeliever?

RAISE UP THE NEXT GENERATION OF MINISTRY LEADERS. Lilias's vision for North Africans to come to Christ was larger than her own life. As she aged, she was intentional to train new foreign missionaries, as well as local Algerian ministry leaders, so the gospel work she started would continue after she was gone.

The apostle Paul, too, was careful to raise up a new generation of gospel workers beyond himself. He calls Timothy his true child in the faith (1 Tim. 1:2) and had Timothy accompany him on his missionary journeys (Acts 16:3). In addition, Paul's letters are replete with instructions for ministry leaders.

Read 2 Timothy 4:1–8. What are Paul's charges to Timothy through verse 7? And what does Paul reflect on in verses 6–8? Who is your mother or father in the faith, and how did they invest in you? Who is your child or children in the faith? As you think about your role in the kingdom, how are you training up the next generation to carry the mantle after you're gone?

Hannah More: Steadfast in Controversy

KAREN SWALLOW PRIOR

From 1799 to 1803, in the little lakeside village of Blagdon, nestled along the gently sloping hills of Somerset County, England, a controversy roiled. Flyers plastered the roadway into town, rudely mocking the figures at the center of the furor. Clergymen from country parishes and city cathedrals staked out their positions. Villagers, fearing the repercussions, avoided making the "wrong" associations. Several national newspapers weighed in, adding to hundreds of pages of pamphlets and letters published on the debate. False and malicious rumors of illicit love affairs and charges of treason swirled around the pious woman everyone seemed to be talking about.[1]

---

1   Unless otherwise noted, this chapter is adapted from my book *Fierce Convictions: The Extraordinary Life of Hannah More — Poet, Reformer, Abolitionist* (Nashville: Thomas Nelson, 2014).

Who was this woman stirring up ire from one side and admiration from the other? She was Hannah More, a longtime Christian educator, activist, and abolitionist, who, ironically, abhorred more than anything else faction, division, and strife.

. . .

Hannah bridged many divides during her lifetime. Born poor, she gained access to the most elite circles of her day. As a woman in a man's world, she achieved things few women before her had achieved. As a lifelong member of the Church of England and an evangelical, her faith gave her a heart for friendship with people of different beliefs. Despite being conservative both theologically and politically, Hannah would not settle for the status quo; instead, she worked toward much needed social reforms and greater flourishing for all.

To that end, Hannah had opened a Sunday school in Blagdon, one of a dozen similar schools she had established across the region. Like other Sunday schools during this time (before the institution of public education), the school offered free, basic academic instruction to poor children of the village on Sundays, the only day when the laborers, including young children, ceased from their work. Hannah's schools taught the children (and eventually adults) to read, do arithmetic, recite the catechism, and practice basic skills that could lead them to better employment. By this time, more than 1,500 students were attending her schools across ten different parishes, with that number ever increasing.[2] With remarkable grit, Hannah and her sister Patty (her closest companion) traversed the countryside on horseback as they sought local support for each school they opened, found teachers to hire, enticed the village children to attend, and oversaw the schools once they were up and running. The sisters'

2   James A. Huie, *Records of Female Piety* (Edinburgh: Oliver and Boyd, 1841), 295–296.

exertions bore tremendous fruit, with each village seeing souls converted, congregations filled, newly skilled workers hired, and income among poor families increased.

Yet, despite all the good the schools were accomplishing, not everyone supported the project. In Blagdon, a perfect storm of cultural, political, and ecclesiastical crosswinds led to the greatest crisis of Hannah's life, one the village is remembered for even today, and an event in church history from which we can still learn.

FRACTURED WORLD

In late-18th-century Britain, the nation felt vulnerable. It had just lost a war against the American colonies. Another revolution, one even more violent, had just taken place across the channel in France. In a hierarchical society such as this one, people in power feared that any effort to teach the poor to read would inevitably lead to revolution. These fears also provided convenient cover for more selfish motives: the labors of the poor were a ready resource for landowners who stood to lose a lot if members of the laboring class became less easy to exploit.

Beyond socio-political opposition to the schools, Hannah More faced obstacles from within the church. Legitimate doctrinal and ecclesiastical issues were at play in the Blagdon Controversy, as it came to be called. This was a time of heightened sensitivity toward schism and dissension in the Church of England. The democratizing influence of the evangelical movement, led earlier in the century by John and Charles Wesley, was gaining traction, threatening to splinter the denomination that had united the nation for two and a half centuries. Any church practice or approach that strayed beyond the clear doctrines and teachings of the Church of England or the *Book of Common Prayer* was suspected of links to "Wesleyism" or "Methodism" (how many referred to evangelicalism).

Unfortunately, the teacher Hannah had hired for the Blagdon school engaged in practices that didn't adhere strictly to the Church of England. These included leading extemporaneous prayer (beyond the prayers in the *Book of Common Prayer)* and seeking personal testimonies of faith — practices common among evangelicals today, but considered strange and even cultish by some in those days. Furthermore, while living in Bath, Hannah once took communion at the nearby church of William Jay, a dissenting minister whose congregation was not part of the Church of England — a questionable act for an Anglican that further fueled attacks against Hannah's orthodoxy.

Moreover, while Hannah had the strong support of the most important church leaders of the time, not all men (including the curate of the Blagdon parish) were eager to see a woman exert as much authority as Hannah did, even in contexts outside the church. Hannah's schools had the approval of the church hierarchy, and some critics, rather than being assuaged, were inflamed by jealousy and resentment. Indeed, one biographer argues that the entire controversy was rooted in sexism since Hannah was "the embodiment of a revisionist female ideology," "an activist model"[3] that was replacing the traditional ideal of women as "accommodating" (particularly within a theologically conservative context).

Such a mixture of legitimate doctrinal disagreements with various power plays clouded the issues, making it harder for people of good faith to know the truth and increasing the speculation and drama. It made Hannah an easy target for various kinds of critics on all sides of the doctrinal and political divides. Hannah's reform efforts, although based on sound doctrine and biblical Christianity, threatened the old, stable categories. In earlier years, things hadn't been so polarized and fraught, and ecumenical associations weren't so risky. The world around Hannah, including the church, was growing more politicized, frightened, and territorial — but she was not.

3   Anne Stott, "Hannah More and the Blagdon Controversy, 1799–1802," *The Journal of Ecclesiastical History,* 51.2 (April 2000), 319–346.

Perhaps it helped Hannah to always have been somewhat of an outsider: too female in a male-dominated society, too prim for high society, too devout in a culture of nominal Christianity. It was Hannah's fate to often feel like a square peg in a round hole. But in his providence, God used Hannah's ill-fittedness to stretch the contours of her world — as well as herself — increasingly into his likeness.

CHRISTIANITY, PRACTICAL AND PURE

For the next few years, as the Blagdon Controversy continued to rage, Hannah was denounced publicly, cruelly, and thoroughly, along with her four sisters, her lifelong help and support. The flyers posted along the road pointed passersby to where they could find a "menagerie of five female savages of the most desperate kind."[4] Critics accused Hannah not only of "Methodism" and "disloyalty" to her church and her country, but, astonishingly, of "not believing one word of Christianity."[5] Some of the worst attacks came from clergymen and were often based on her sex. She was derogatively referred to as a "she-bishop" and a "bishop in petticoats." One minister even adopted a pseudonym — "Reverend Sir Archibald Macsarcasm" — in order to publish page after page of vicious lies about her.

Ultimately, Hannah was vindicated. The church hierarchy stood by her, and that made all the difference. But the school didn't survive. Hannah chose to close it in order not to risk harm to the rest of the schools.

---

4   As quoted in Jeremy and Margaret Collingwood, *Hannah More* (Oxford: Lion Publishing, 1990), 97.

5   Henry Thompson, *The Life of Hannah More, with Notices of her Sisters* (London: Cadell, 1838), 93.

When it was all over, Hannah collapsed emotionally, spiritually, and physically. She had consistently struggled with bouts of illness; many of her symptoms at various time evidenced what we understand today to be clinical depression. But the aftermath of this controversy became what she later called her "great illness," lasting from 1803 to 1805. She had been attacked, she felt, "with a wantonness of cruelty which, in civilized places, few persons, especially of my sex, have been called to suffer."[6] On July 8, 1803, she wrote in her diary, "My very soul is sick of religious controversy. Christianity is a broad basis. Bible Christianity is what I love ... a Christianity practical and pure, which teaches holiness, humility, repentance and faith in Christ; and which after summing up all the Evangelical graces, declares that the greatest of these is charity."[7]

LOVER OF EDUCATION

After Christ and the church, Hannah More loved education more than anything else. She had been a precocious learner as a young girl taught at home by her father, a charity school master in a quiet village outside the city of Bristol. In 1745, the year Hannah was born, Bristol was a bustling city, its sea ports producing tremendous wealth for its citizens as a result of the growing trade in African imports — including human slaves. Yet in God's divine providence, Hannah turned the opportunities the city provided her into gifts she could use to fight that evil trade and bring the reforming message of the gospel to the nation.

Hannah was the fourth of the Mores's five surviving children, all girls. After her older sisters opened a school for girls in Bristol, Hannah joined them, first as a student, then as a teacher. When

---

6   William Roberts, *The Life and Correspondence of Mrs. Hannah More, 2 vols.* (New York: Harper & Brothers, 1834), 2.56.
7   Ibid., 2.111.

Hannah became engaged to a wealthy gentleman whose young cousins attended the school, it seemed her path had taken a delightful turn. But the wedding never took place. After several years of repeated stalling, the reluctant suitor finally released Hannah from their betrothal and settled an annuity on her (as was customary in such situations). Hannah was heartbroken and overcome by the shame of rejection. But as was the pattern for the rest of her life, after allowing herself time to recover, she turned to the next thing. And that next thing, now that she had financial independence, was to go to London to make her way as a writer.

In 1774, Hannah left her teaching post at the school and made the two-day journey to London with two of her sisters. From a young age, she had been writing poetry and drama, and some of her work had made its way to London before she arrived. Hannah was welcomed warmly there within the most prestigious literary and artistic circles, befriending such luminaries as the critic Samuel Johnson, the painter Sir Joshua Reynolds, the conservative statesman Edmund Burke, the bluestocking Elizabeth Montagu, and the stage producer David Garrick, who produced two of Hannah's plays for the London stage. The many letters written between Hannah and her family and friends offer colorful details of dinner parties, theater outings, and lively conversations. Yet the letters also show that the young woman who was poor by birth and pious by nature never felt fully comfortable in fashionable society.

BATTLING WITH HER PEN

In 1780, a friend gave Hannah a devotional book written by John Newton, the famous former slave ship captain who had become a clergyman and hymnist (and author of "Amazing Grace"). In reading this work, something happened in Hannah's heart and mind. She had always been an observant, devout Christian, but Newton's testimony of God's saving and sanctifying grace in these pages led Hannah over the next several years to fully commit her soul and talents to the Lord and to reclaiming society for his kingdom.

In 1787, Hannah went to hear Newton preach at his church. They talked together afterward for an hour, and when she left, her "pockets were stuffed full of sermons."[8] The same year Hannah met Newton's young protégé, William Wilberforce, the Parliament member who would lead the campaign to abolish the British slave trade over the next few decades. Wilberforce encouraged Hannah not to retire from the world as she was contemplating doing, but rather to leverage the fame she had gained through her literary accomplishments for greater good. Wilberforce told Hannah, "More is to be done out of the House [of Commons] than in it." In other words, while Wilberforce and others would battle against the slave trade through politics, Hannah More would battle it with her pen.

In 1788, Hannah published the poem "Slavery," coinciding with a resolution Wilberforce planned to introduce to Parliament restricting the number of slaves that could be put on slave ships. Such legislation fell far short of the goal of complete abolition. But the group of evangelicals known as the Clapham Sect, which included Hannah and Wilberforce, had a long-term, multi-pronged approach for broad social reform — a plan that proved successful. Hannah's poem was praised far and wide (and is included in many literature anthologies today). It is said to have helped inspire the missionaries of the next century, such as David Livingston, to take the gospel to Africa.

In addition to *Slavery*, More wrote numerous other abolitionist literary works. She was also a prolific letter writer and shared heartbreaking testimonies of the trade with many correspondents, those accounts she had heard from eye witnesses at the many dinners, social events, and abolitionist meetings she attended. She even led

8   Collingwood, *Hannah More*, 59.

one of the first and most effective boycotts of West Indian sugar, a staple of the British culture and economy.

TEACHING A NATION TO READ

In the middle of this daunting effort to abolish slavery (an effort that would not succeed for 40 years), Hannah began the Sunday schools, inspired and funded by her friend Wilberforce, who had witnessed the misery of village laborers while visiting Hannah in her country home near Cheddar's famous cliffs. "Something must be done for Cheddar," he insisted. "If you will be at the trouble," Wilberforce promised, "I will be at the expense." They stayed up late that night — Wilberforce, Hannah, and her sister Patty — and finally hatched a plan to open a school.[9] Over the next few years, they opened a dozen such schools across the region — including the one at the center of the Blagdon Controversy.

But it wasn't only the schools that earned Hannah the credit for teaching her nation to read. Just as in earlier years she had written treatises for the rich and fashionable (which had been widely and well received), she wrote now for new audiences that spanned all of British society (and indeed reached many far places in the world). When she realized there was a dearth of good reading material for the newly literate, she turned, once again, to her pen. From 1795 to 1798, Hannah oversaw a repository of inexpensive tracts containing lively tales, songs, and lessons to engage the imaginations of developing readers and teach them in matters of religion, virtue, and domestic economy. Then, with novels becoming all the rage among middle-class readers, she wrote her own novel — a story celebrating sound education and a Christian view of marriage — which, upon its

---

9   *Mendip Annals: Or, A Narrative of the Charitable Labours of Hannah and Martha More in Their Neighbourhood: Being the Journal of Martha More,* reprint (London: James Nisbet and Co., 1859), 12–13.

publication in 1809, became one of the first bestsellers in English
literature. Over the years, she wrote several treatises on education,
including one for Princess Charlotte that was read by the royal family. It is fortunate for the world that she followed the advice given to
her by John Wesley through one of her sisters, exhorting her to write
for those who would not listen to preachers: "Tell her to live in the
world; there is the sphere of her usefulness; they will not let us come
nigh them."[10]

As Hannah grew older — and wealthier — her writings and activities focused less on social reform and more on spiritual growth,
discipleship, and the Bible. The beautiful country estate she purchased outside the village of Wrington in 1801 — which had been
her refuge during the Blagdon Controversy — became a destination
for Christian pilgrims from all over England (and even America) who
wanted to learn from her. The poet Samuel T. Coleridge was among
her visitors, as were a number of young clergymen-in-training whom
Hannah supported financially.

FAITHFUL TO THE END

During all these years, Hannah continued to press for the end of
slavery, alongside her friend William Wilberforce and many other
faithful abolitionists. Finally, on July 26, 1833, the Emancipation
Bill passed in the House of Commons, decreeing that all slaves in
the British Empire were to be freed within one year. Wilberforce
died three days later. One month later, the House of Lords passed
the Slavery Abolition Act. On September 6, 1833, two months after
Wilberforce's death, Hannah joined Wilberforce — along with all
four of her sisters who had gone before her — in heavenly glory.

Although she had received one or two proposals after the broken engagement of her youth, Hannah never married. She never had

10   Roberts, *The Life and Correspondence of Mrs. Hannah More*, 2.323.

children. Born to a lowly charity school master, she died in 1833 a wealthy woman, leaving most of her money to Christian charities, schools, and mission societies in England, America, and across the world. Despite her name being largely forgotten, Hannah More's legacy is large and lasting. She helped free slaves, taught the poor to read, and encouraged her nation toward genuine Christianity. Most important, she was faithful to the end.

LESSONS FROM THE FAITHFUL

What we can learn about steadfast endurance from Hannah More

EXPECT OPPOSITION WHEN YOU ARE FAITHFUL. The hardest opposition Hannah More faced was from others within the church. Some of that opposition was rooted in doctrinal differences and concerns; but some seemed to oppose her out of sinful fears or desires. Most opposition was probably a mixture of good and sinful motivations. How discouraged, confused, and hurt Hannah must have been — and we feel the same when we face similar trials, whether from our brothers and sisters in Christ or from outside the church.

We are all fallen, and we live in a fallen world. To be human means we will face opposition — sometimes because our opponents are wrong, sometimes because we are, and usually because none will do a perfect thing in a perfect way. Even believers can misunderstand one another, disagree, and give in to sinful temptations. To be a Christian serving the Lord means we have a spiritual enemy as well. Furthermore, the enemy can use divisions within the body of Christ even more powerfully than those we have within the world. But being a faithful, wise Christian means resisting the temptation to think that opposition will come only from the world and not from fellow believers. All opposition can be used by God refine us, test our faithfulness, and develop our wisdom and maturity.

Read 1 Peter 2. Verse 12 cautions against what response to fiery trials? What does this verse say is the purpose of such trials? How does verse 15 tell us we can "put to silence the ignorance of foolish people"?

DISCERN WHICH CRITICISM IS WORTH LISTENING TO — AND WHICH ISN'T. One of Hannah More's character flaws was that she was a people pleaser. She often lacked confidence — and not without good reason. After all, she rose well above the station she was born into, which was unusual for the time, and lacked many of the privileges that people in her circles possessed, owing solely to their birth. Some of the criticism she faced came from cattiness, jealousy, fear, competition, and even weak Christianity.

On the other hand, Hannah sometimes took risks that reaped consequences that might otherwise have been avoided. For example, there was nothing wrong with the teacher at her school praying an unscripted prayer (something evangelicals today take for granted). Yet, because she needed the support of her own denomination to establish the schools, it was risky for her to hire a teacher whom (as her letters show) she knew to practice outside the rigid bonds of Anglican orthodoxy, an expectation of the day. By the time the Blagdon Controversy was over, she heeded the criticism by closing the school. It was a compromise, given her understanding of prayer and personal faith, but it was likely the wisest course of action to pay attention to her critics and, in so doing, to respect the church leaders whom she knew were striving to balance difficult tensions during a tumultuous period of history.

We can learn a great deal from our critics. Wisdom consists of discerning which criticism offers helpful truths for us to learn from — and which will serve only to distract, dissuade, or discourage us.

Read 1 John 4:1. When we test the spirit behind our critics, what should be looking for? Why? What measure do we use to make this assessment? Is there a particular criticism you need to discern as helpful or unhelpful, true or untrue, today?

RECOGNIZE HOW DIFFICULT IT IS TO SEE PAST TODAY'S CUL-
TURAL LENS AND THROUGH THE LENS OF BIBLICAL UNDER-
STANDING. Many white Europeans and Americans of the 18th and
19th centuries rationalized human slavery. A few looked beyond this
cultural lens, seeing slavery's evil for what it was. Hannah More and
her friends were among these.

Most of us tend to think that if we lived then, we would be
among the few — but we ought not to be so confident in ourselves.
It is exceedingly difficult to see past our cultural framework in order
to comprehend eternal and universal truth. We are like the goldfish
in the bowl who, when asked by the cat, "How's the water?" responds in puzzlement, "What water?" The Bible offers us the way
to see past cultural and social norms (although only "darkly" as
Paul says in 1 Cor. 13:12). Even so, there has never been a society
in which egregious wrongs have not been accepted as normal. Ours
is no exception. Yet it is easy to look upon past eras and think that
we would never have been so wicked or vile as to accept their evil
practices. We cannot know for sure, and this humbles us.

*Read Proverbs 14:12. What are some past norms that people of
those times accepted too easily? What are cultural norms today that
clearly go against Scripture? Think about some ways that Christians can
learn from the past and cultivate humility in the present. Is there any
issue that other Christians are speaking against today that you do not
find problematic? Could they be right and you be wrong?*

Joni Eareckson Tada: Steadfast in Pain

VANEETHA RENDALL RISNER

Joni's signature earrings are hammered gold, with crinkled edges that almost sparkle. They were once smooth polished squares, an unexpected gift from a dear friend after Joni had admired them. She wore them constantly, but one day at work, one slipped off her ear. As Joni wheeled to get help, she heard a sickening crunch — her treasured earring had been crushed by the wheelchair tire.

Joni took the earring to a local jeweler who said it couldn't be fixed; the damage was too great. He did, however, offer to alter the smooth one to match the other. Joni was hesitant to potentially ruin these beautiful earrings, but she decided to trust him. As she waited, she heard pounding and grinding from the back and wondered if the jeweler knew what he was doing. Soon, he returned with a matching second gold earring. It was marred and mangled, but strangely magnificent, resembling the work of a skilled craftsmen. The hammering had produced something breathtaking.

Those earrings have become a metaphor for Joni's life. God knows what he's doing as he hammers and shapes and bends his people to better reflect his glory.

. . .

Joni Eareckson was born to John and Lindy Eareckson, the youngest of four daughters, on October 15, 1949 in Baltimore, Maryland.
Since her parents were convinced that she was going to be a boy,
they named her after her father, but gladly changed the spelling to
Joni (pronounced "Johnny") when she was born. From the beginning, athletics were important in the Eareckson home as John had
been an alternate on the 1932 Olympic wrestling team and was later
named to the National Wrestling Hall of Fame. Joni herself was vot-
ed best athlete in her senior class; she loved all sports from tennis to
swimming to horseback riding.[1]

After a stirring talk at Young Life camp her sophomore year
of high school, Joni committed her life to Christ. At first, her new
faith brought conviction and repentance, but soon her interest in
God was relegated to Christian activities like singing in the church
choir and attending Young Life meetings. Worse yet, her fragile faith
was further diminished by making one immoral choice after another.[2] Discouraged by her apathy and sin, she wrote on the back of an
index card, "I'm tired of saying I'm a Christian out of one side of my
mouth and saying something else out of the other. I want to honor
God with my life. And so God, I'm asking you to please, please do
something in my life to turn it around, because I'm making a mess of
it . . . "[3]

1   Joni Eareckson Tada, *Joni: An Unforgettable Story* (Grand Rapids: Zondervan,
     (1976), 2012), 32–33.
2   Ibid., 36–44.
3   Joni Eareckson Tada, *The God I Love: A Lifetime of Walking with Jesus* (Grand
     Rapids: Zondervan, 2003), 144.

DEFINING CRISIS

On July 30, 1967, Joni went to the beach with her sister, Kathy, and dove off the pier into the Chesapeake Bay. Her head immediately collided with a hard surface, and Joni's body sprawled out of control. She desperately tried to move her limbs but couldn't. Unable to breathe and on the verge of losing consciousness, Joni was trapped motionless as she lay face down in the water. At the same moment, a crab bit Kathy, who turned to tell Joni what had happened. Kathy then noticed her sister floating eerily still, with only her blonde hair visible. Kathy rushed over to Joni and, with the help of friends, pulled her sister onto a nearby raft. Within minutes the ambulance arrived and sped off to the hospital.

At the emergency room, Joni had no idea what had happened. Doctors and nurses busied themselves with her care, but no one told her anything. She soon learned that she had severed her spinal cord, rendering her a quadriplegic, paralyzed from the shoulders down. She would spend the next few months in a steel Stryker frame, alternating between lying face up looking at the ceiling or facedown staring at the floor. Convinced that her paralysis was temporary and that she would eventually walk again, Joni prayed continuously for strength and healing. Over the years, countless people would pray over her, assuring Joni that she just needed enough faith to be healed. Joni did believe, but as her body remained paralyzed, her faith began to weaken. It seemed impossible that a good and sovereign God would deny her healing.[4]

---

4   Tada, *Joni,* 17–31, 74–75.

QUESTIONING GOD'S GOODNESS

Convinced that God would do a miracle, Joni went to a healing crusade, hoping this could be her chance to walk. But when the leader didn't even turn to the wheelchair section, Joni wondered why a healer would not hear the prayers of people with disabilities.[5] As the months dragged on, hopelessness set in. Joni wanted to die; life wasn't worth living if she couldn't use her hands and feet. She begged friends to help her end her life since she couldn't even do that herself. She finally cried out to God in desperation, "God, I can't live like this. If you won't let me die, then show me how to live ... "[6] Unknown to Joni, God was already answering her prayer.

Joni's friend Steve Estes, a teenager himself, began visiting Joni at home, spending hours talking with her about the Bible. She had many questions, and Steve patiently listened, searching the Scriptures with her for answers. One afternoon, Joni asked Steve, "How can a good God allow so much suffering? If he's all loving, then how in the world can permanent and lifelong paralysis be a part of his loving plan for my life?" Steve responded by pointing out that God allowed Christ to be betrayed by Judas, beaten by mocking soldiers and crucified by Pilate — actions that he clearly would have hated — because it was part of God's larger plan of salvation.[7]

Steve said, "God permits things that he hates — really hates — to accomplish something he loves." He explained that everything that led to the crucifixion of Christ was part of God's will so that, through the cross, the floodgates of heaven would open wide, that whosoever will might come in. Steve pointed out how God "allowed the devil to instigate the Crucifixion all because he had in

---

5   Tada, *The God I Love*, 195.
6   Joni Eareckson Tada, *A Lifetime of Wisdom: Embracing the Way God Heals You* (Grand Rapids: Zondervan, 2009), 28.
7   Tada, *The God I Love*, 217–218.

mind our good."[8] As Steve's words sank in, Joni could see how God could use her disability both for her good and for his glory. Though the disability itself was grueling, the result would be God's best for her life, God's Plan A.

SEEING WITH NEW EYES

Joni's conversation with Steve was a turning point. She later acknowledged to Steve that she was starting to see her injury not as a tragedy but as a gift from God, certain that her wheelchair could become an instrument of joy. Though she still desired healing, her focus was that, through her disability, God would bring glory to himself. She saw how it was already making her more Christlike. She was more patient with her sisters and friends who helped her, humbly admitting that she had been demanding and unappreciative at times. She developed a sour taste for the sins that, beforehand, had seemed so enticing. She started taking every thought captive to the obedience of Christ, understanding that sin was not just what she did but also what she thought.[9] She became steadfast in her suffering, marked by peace and inner contentment. She approached others who had disabilities with compassion, empathizing with their deep pain and longing to reach out to them.

When she was in rehab, therapists urged Joni to learn independence and even start writing using her mouth. But Joni resisted; to her it was degrading. Eventually, however, she learned to write, and even started painting, by holding a brush in her mouth. Joni's artwork was extraordinary — her talent got the attention of a local gallery who persuaded her to do a showing of her paintings. The

8   Ibid., 218.
9   Tada, *Joni*, 132–138.

response to this showing was overwhelming and led to an interview with Barbara Walters on the *TODAY Show*.[10]

OVERNIGHT SUCCESS

Soon after the interview, people encouraged Joni to write her life story, and in 1976, her autobiography *Joni* was published. The book was an instant success, and Billy Graham asked Joni to accompany him on several crusades where she was able to speak to enormous crowds. She often ended her stirring talks saying, "Even paralyzed people can walk with the Lord."[11] In 1979, a feature film on Joni's life, starring Joni herself, garnered instant acclaim and was viewed by millions worldwide. As the letters poured in, Joni realized she needed to offer people eternal hope in Christ, not just a letter in response, so she founded Joni and Friends (JAF), her ministry serving people with disabilities and their families.[12] This ministry sends wheelchairs around the world, offering gospel hope and tangible help for people who are disabled. JAF also offers family retreats to encourage both the disabled and also their loved ones, who are often weary from the day-to-day struggles of caregiving. Joni's personal ministry, to encourage and support the struggling, has touched countless people through her books, speaking, and radio program. Her driving message has always been, "Jesus is ecstasy beyond

---

10   Ibid., 82, 91–96, 174–184.
11   Tada, *The God I Love*, 221.
12   Joni Eareckson Tada, "Why I Started Joni & Friends," Joni and Friends, August 2, 2019, https://www.joniandfriends.org/why-i-started-joni-and-friends/.

compare, and it's worth anything to be his friend, even if it means a wheelchair."[13]

NEW CHAPTER: MARRIAGE

As Joni's ministry was taking off, Ken Tada was watching from the sidelines. In 1980, Joni and Ken met after a service at Grace Community Church and then bumped into each other everywhere. Joni was bedridden with pressure sores when Ken came to visit for the first time, bringing an easel that he created so she could paint in bed. He was serious about winning her heart — and soon he did just that.[14] Much as she loved being with Ken, Joni wasn't sure if he, or any man, would be able to handle the day-to-day burdens of marrying someone with quadriplegia. But Ken was undeterred, secure that his love for Joni and the Lord would give him the necessary strength. So, on July 3, 1982, Ken and Joni were married. On the day of their wedding, as Joni was wheeling down the aisle, her flowers tumbled to the side, and her wheelchair tires left tracks on her beautiful gown. After the service, Joni told Ken of her disappointment, wondering if he had noticed the imperfections as well. Ken laughed as he said, "No, I thought you were gorgeous."[15] While Joni had seen the things that weren't perfect, Ken was looking to something much greater: the beauty of his bride.

Even before the wedding, they began their ministry together, journeying around the world and spreading the message of God's love and faithfulness. Their first major trip in spring 1982 was to

---

13   Joni Eareckson Tada, "Reflections on the 50th Anniversary of My Diving Accident," The Gospel Coalition, July 30, 2017, https://www.thegospelcoalition. org/article/reflections-on-50th-anniversary-of-my-diving-accident/.

14   Ken and Joni Eareckson Tada with Larry Libby, *Joni & Ken: An Untold Love Story* (Grand Rapids: Zondervan, 2013), 36–50.

15   Ibid., 74.

Romania, where leaders insisted they had no disabled in their country, almost daring the couple to find someone in a wheelchair. Their words were true — there were no visible wheelchairs — because the disabled were shunned, forced to live in hiding, or even euthanized. In 1989, after the Iron Curtain fell, Joni and Ken had the opportunity to return to Eastern Europe with Billy Graham's historic crusade in Hungary, where Joni spoke to 110,000 people.[16] Thousands came forward to commit their lives to Christ, as they wanted to know this God who sustains in suffering and uses pain in bigger ways than we can understand.

ANOTHER TRIAL: CHRONIC PAIN

While quadriplegia required a constant battle of dying to self, depending on others, and submitting to God, Joni said she had become "used to" paralysis. What she could not get "used to" was the new and unexpected suffering that began in 2001.[17] Without warning, Joni felt a sharp pain originating in her left hip which turned into a driving pain that never relented, night or day, often leaving her breathless and writhing in agony. She said, "I used to pray for grace to maximize each day; now I pray for survival."[18]

Through this pain, Joni was relearning utter dependence on God. She had made peace with quadriplegia decades earlier, but *this* — how does one come to terms with chronic, jagged pain that makes even sleep elusive? Joni was speaking to a class about this latest development when a student asked her, "Why do you think

16   Tada, *The God I Love*, 258–271.
17   Joni Eareckson Tada, *A Place of Healing: Wrestling with the Mysteries of Suffering, Pain, and God's Sovereignty* (Colorado Springs: David C Cook, 2010), 24.
18   Ibid., 154.

God allowed this?" Joni paused as tears welled up in her eyes. This question, asked as she was experiencing razor-sharp pain, brought her again to the familiar question of *why*. Joni answered, "Why? I don't know. Maybe — maybe He has allowed this so that what you've just heard — the last 45 minutes — wouldn't come off as something trite, something rehearsed, or sound like a platitude."[19] Those who have suffered, and are living in pain, can teach us the deepest lessons about God and his sufficiency. Joni's agony made her message more real: she wasn't giving lessons learned long ago, but lessons she was learning right then, in front of them, within the fire.

LESSONS FROM PAIN

To prepare her body for rest, Joni needed to go to bed several hours before she could fall asleep. This could have felt like wasted time, but Joni chose to pray and intercede for others, certain that God had ordained this time for his glory. Soon after she fell asleep, Joni would awaken in agony, lying alert in bed for hours. Yet, rather than feel sorry for herself, Joni would once again pray and worship God, aware that the spiritual realm was watching her and that her response to her suffering mattered. Joni wanted her life to be a blackboard upon which God could chalk lessons about himself.[20]

At the True Woman 2010 conference, Joni said that she had been lying awake in bed at 2 a.m. and then realized,

> Something unseen and electrifying is abuzz in my dark room. The unseen world and all the heavenly host including powers

---

19 Ibid., 24.

20 Vaneetha Rendall Risner, "Joni Eareckson Tada: 'Don't Deny Christ. The Stakes Are Too High,'" Christianity Today (formerly Today's Christian Woman), November 2015, https://www.christianitytoday.com/women/2015/november/joni-eareckson-tada-dont-deny-christ-stakes-are-too-high.html.

and principalities are watching me. They are listening to me and as I respond, they are learning about God and his character through me. I can't tell you how many times I've been able to press on because I know my life is on display. We don't suffer for nothing and we never suffer alone ... My response to hardship is never isolated. It isn't true that no one cares or notices. The stakes are high and God's reputation is on the line. It's all for God's glory ... "[21]

While Joni's pain was like a tornado ripping through her life, it was flattening Ken as well. He felt helpless as he watched Joni suffer. Moreover, Ken had been an outdoorsman and an athlete, and Joni's care was taking a toll on him. The day-and-night drudgery of Joni's disability routine — including emptying her leg bag and occasionally getting urine on his fingers, picking up her medications, hassling with insurance companies, and doing all the household chores, while living in the shadow of Joni's fame — was a lonely burden.[22] Additionally, he now woke up several times during the night to turn Joni when her pain became unbearable. Ken was sinking into a depression, and frequently contemplated suicide.[23] He began retreating into himself, letting others provide much of Joni's care as he was

21   Joni Eareckson Tada, "The Stakes Are Higher than You Think," Revive Our Hearts, filmed September 20, 2010 at True Woman 2010, https://www.reviveourhearts.com/events/true-woman-10-indianapolis/stakes-are-higher-you-think/.

22   Tada, *Joni & Ken*, 84.

23   Ibid., 110.

struggling to stay alive. Judy, Joni's lifelong friend and assistant, took on an even greater role as her main caregiver and support.

YET ANOTHER TRIAL: CANCER

With no reprieve in sight, Joni and Ken were drifting apart, each dealing with their own private pain. Yet another trial emerged when, in 2010, Joni found a lump in her breast that they learned was Stage 3 cancer. Joni accepted the news gracefully, but behind closed doors reality crashed upon her. She couldn't believe that she had to face cancer and surgery layered upon her endless pain and paralysis. She collapsed into tears, worried that this diagnosis would plummet Ken deeper into depression.[24]

Much to everyone's surprise, this trial somehow restored Ken's love and fierceness for Joni that had been buried by years of daily duties. Ken had recently undergone a spiritual awakening, sensing that God was preparing him for this diagnosis. He knew God would give him the strength to care for his precious wife.[25]

Judy was there with Joni and Ken when they received the news about her cancer. Since Judy was a nurse, she often handled the medical issues with Joni, but this time, Ken stepped in. "Let me take over,"[26] he said, and he did. He was by Joni's side when she underwent a radical mastectomy and remained there during all of her chemotherapy and radiation appointments. These treatments were intense, leaving Joni nauseous and unable to throw up without someone turning her onto her side. On top of that, Joni developed pneumonia, which is often deadly for quadriplegics. Yet, by God's grace, Joni recovered and was declared cancer-free five years later. Through that ordeal, their marriage became stronger

24   Ibid., 34.
25   Ibid., 130–136.
26   Ibid., 34.

as God gave Ken a new vision and direction for his calling and their joint ministry.

JONI'S LEGACY

Joni had a recurrence of cancer in 2018, but after radiation, doctors have found no further evidence of cancer at the writing of this chapter. She still lives with chronic pain; yet her life shines for Jesus in remarkable ways. Joni tirelessly spreads the message of suffering and God's glory and to date has written more than 50 books, many of which have won awards. In 2003, she received the Gold Medallion Lifetime Achievement Award for her writing. Today, she hosts *Joni and Friends* and *Diamonds in the Dust,* two short inspirational daily radio programs; she has served on numerous advisory committees, including the National Council on Disability; and she has been interviewed on countless television programs such as *Larry King Live* and *ABC News*. Additionally, she has traveled worldwide, delivering wheelchairs and ministering to families in more than 47 countries. Joni has given her life to glorify God and spread the message of hope in suffering through Christ.[27]

DEEPER HEALING IN CHRIST

While Joni begged for healing in the early years of her paralysis, God has used her suffering in ways she could never have imagined. In her devotional, *Beside Bethesda,* Joni recounts her words to the Lord

---

27   Joni Eareckson Tada, "Joni's Corner," Joni and Friends, https://old.joniand-friends.org/jonis-corner/jonis-bio/.

during a trip she and Ken made to Israel. While visiting the pool of Bethesda in Jerusalem, she said to him through tears:

> Thank you for the healing that you gave me, the deeper healing. Oh God, you were so wise in not giving me a physical healing. You were so wise because a "no" answer to a physical healing has meant "yes" to a deeper faith in you. "Yes" to a deeper prayer life. "Yes" to a greater understanding of your word. It has purged sin from my life, forced me to depend on your grace, increased my compassion for others who hurt, put complaining behind me, stretched my hope, given me a lively and buoyant trust in you and an excitement about heaven, pushed me to give thanks in times of sorrow, increased my faith and helped me to love you more. Jesus, I love you more.[28]

Joni Eareckson Tada's life shines brightly for the Lord. She has endured near-relentless suffering — but she has remained steadfast, inspiring millions through her faithfulness to love Jesus more.

LESSONS FROM THE FAITHFUL

What we can learn about steadfast endurance from Joni Eareckson Tada

CONSIDER HOW GOD USES SUFFERING FOR GOOD. In the early years of her quadriplegia, Joni and others prayed fervently for her physical healing, yet she remained paralyzed. In her prayer by the pool of Bethesda, she details the deeper healing that God has given her through her affliction. He has used it for good in numerous ways.

In our society, we avoid suffering — running from it if we can and numbing its effects if we can't. The prosperity gospel has even

---

28   Joni Eareckson Tada, *Beside Bethesda: 31 Days Toward Deeper Healing* (Colorado Springs: NavPress, 2014), 168–169.

promoted the wrong ideas to Christians, teaching that faithfulness to God will result in a prosperous and pain-free life. But this false gospel discounts the ways that God uses suffering for good: stronger character, deeper faith, and greater compassion.

Read Romans 5:3–5 and 2 Corinthians 12:7–10. How can suffering be good for us? What blessings does God give us in suffering? What has God done in your life through suffering that you can be thankful for?

ENCOURAGE OTHERS THROUGH YOUR SUFFERING. God gave Joni a message of hope through her physical suffering, one that has been shared all over the world. As a result, she began the ministry Joni and Friends to serve people with disabilities and their families. Joni was able to turn her suffering into an opportunity to care for others who are struggling.

Like Joni, people who have suffered understand the unique needs of those who are going through something similar, whether it be dealing with the loss of a loved one, difficult health issues, or relational problems.

Read 2 Corinthians 1:3–4. What happens after we receive God's comfort in our suffering? How might God use your particular struggles to encourage others who are going through similar pain? Is there anyone you can encourage and comfort today?

REALIZE THAT YOUR RESPONSE TO SUFFERING MATTERS FOR GOD'S GLORY. Joni is comforted when she wakes up at night in pain, knowing that the angels and demons are observing the way she responds to it. She knows God uses her life as a blackboard on which to chalk lessons about himself. That truth encourages her to press on, since her response matters for his glory.

Often our trials are private, taking place where no one else sees. They may be invisible to outsiders and perhaps too personal to share publicly, making us feel isolated and misunderstood. When no one sees or knows what's happening, we may think that our response to suffering — whether we are faithful or faithless — doesn't matter.

We may forget that God is always with us and is watching, and that the heavenly hosts are watching as well.

Read Ephesians 3:10–13. What does Paul say is one purpose of the church? How does this purpose shed light on the church's response to suffering? Where do you feel that no one sees or understands what you are going through, and how does this Scripture encourage you?

SERVE IN A POWERFUL WAY THROUGH PRAYER. Joni has seen the importance of prayer and has spent countless hours praying for others. She understands that prayer is an essential work in the kingdom of God, and while it is unseen and secret, it is the most powerful and loving thing we can do. Joni is also convinced that prayers offered in times of affliction possess greater power before God's throne because they are sacrificially voiced.

It's easier to serve God in the limelight — when we are publicly praised for our efforts and people are thankful for our work — than it is in the secret places. When people are suffering, whether physically or emotionally, they often wonder how they can be useful to the kingdom, since many outward acts of service are no longer options for them. Yet prayer will always be a most powerful way to serve.

Read James 5:16. Do you regularly pray for those who need strength and healing? If not, make a list of people to pray for now. Commit to regular prayer, specifically crying out to God for the needs of your brothers and sisters, and rest assured that the ministry of prayer is crucial for the body of Christ.

TGC

THE GOSPEL COALITION is a fellowship of evangelical churches deeply committed to renewing our faith in the gospel of Christ and to reforming our ministry practices to conform fully to the Scriptures. We have committed ourselves to invigorating churches with new hope and compelling joy based on the promises received by grace alone through faith alone in Christ alone.

We desire to champion the gospel with clarity, compassion, courage, and joy — gladly linking hearts with fellow believers across denominational, ethnic, and class lines. We yearn to work with all who, in addition to embracing our confession and theological vision for ministry, seek the lordship of Christ over the whole of life with unabashed hope in the power of the Holy Spirit to transform individuals, communities, and cultures.

Through its women's initiatives, The Gospel Coalition aims to support the growth of women in faithfully studying and sharing the Scriptures; in actively loving and serving the church; and in spreading the gospel of Jesus Christ in all their callings.

Join the cause and visit TGC.org for fresh resources that will equip you to love God with all your heart, soul, mind, and strength, and to love your neighbor as yourself.

ALSO AVAILABLE FROM THE GOSPEL COALITION

TGC